Sifting Through
The Ashes

A Seventies Girl Looks Back

Nancy Ingrid Hurd

TESTIMONIALS

"What a poignant writer! Nancy (Hurd) takes us through journeys we've all been through-from our roots, to our difficult decisions to our most cherished moments-with delicacy and inspiration. A masterpiece of emotion that lands us on (our) feet."

Margo Lenmark, Author
Light in the Mourning

"Nancy Hurd has the rare ability to take real life and transform it into words on a page that give the reader the feeling of being there. What a great story she has to tell!"

L.E. Hewitt, Author
My Bucket List Has A Hole In It

"When I recall memories of family and the relationships and bonds grown and tested over time, I am reminded of all the poignant highs and lows that determine the quality and longevity of those relationships. For me, in reading *Sifting Through the Ashes*, Nancy Hurd evoked feelings and emotions I had forgotten about or have tried to ignore. That is a good thing, to remember, and to heal."

Frank Walters Clark, Author & Publisher
Lie Down with Silk and Daggers
Clark Global Publishing

In memory of my beloved son, Neil Andrew Rush, who passed away before this book went into publication.

August 2019

To my Mother, Children and Grandchildren
With Love and Gratitude

"Our lives are at once ordinary and mythical. We live and die, age beautifully or full of wrinkles...we wake in the morning, buy apples and yellow cheese and hope we have enough money to pay for it. At the same instant we have these magnificent hearts that pump through all our sorrow and all the Winters we are alive on the Earth. We are important, and our lives are important...magnificent really...and their details are worthy to be recorded."

Natalie Goldberg

...My heritage

Great, great Uncle "Shelt" Carpenter in his hand-hewn rowboat - Elk River, W.VA

THE GRAND OPENING

I've been thinking lately about my grandfather. He is nearly ninety years old now and the years are beginning to take their toll. Last Summer, Grandpa rowed his canoe down the Monongahela River for the last time. His daughters, my mother and Aunt Carol, were becoming anxious over his lone excursions lest his little boat capsize with no one close around to help him. "Oh, that happens from time to time," he said, not too reassuringly. "I just bob around in the water 'til I can set things right again." A stubborn case of angina has finally put an end to his lifelong fishing career.

But Grandpa never gives up without a fight.

Life was not easy for my grandparents as they raised their family of eight children during the "Great Depression", in the poverty filled coal camps of West Virginia.

Here is a story recently shared with me by my mother from her childhood...

The year was 1938 and Winter was pressing in hard on the family... My Grandfather was a coal miner and a miner's wage at that time was a bit of counterfeit currency called "scrip", which only could be spent at the company store. The miner never received enough "scrip" to adequately cover the needs of his family, so the entirely of his monthly allotment went to the company store, while the remainder of life's necessities, which he could not afford, were placed on his ever-increasing bill. Due to this system the miner truly did, as Tennessee Ernie Ford lamented, "owe his soul to the company store".

There was simply never enough of anything. The Children did not "know" they were poor, since everyone in the community shared their plight, but oh...how acutely my grandparents felt the daily struggle to survive, and anxiety over the welfare of their children.

One evening as Grandpa sat at the kitchen table cutting rubber patches from an old innertube to line the soles of his children's worn-out shoes, he made a decision. He was going to apply for credit with one of the mail-order companies. He was disappointed at being turned down by Sears and Roebuck, but one day received a letter from Montgomery Ward's saying his credit had been approved and a big catalogue accompanied the letter.

My mother still remembers the excitement in their house that night. Even Grandma who had recently lost a two-year-old son to pneumonia, was unusually lighthearted. They sat up late perusing the catalogue and making their final choices. Finally, after much deliberation, the order was sent off...and the wait began.

...Weeks passed. Winter was hard and the snow deep. The long trudge to and from school each day in the bitter cold seemed bearable only because new coats and shoes were coming. Each day on his way home from work, Grandpa searched up and down the railroad track (for the train would never actually stop in their little town, but only slow down to throw a package off) and each day he came home empty handed.

Then one evening a young neighbor boy who was walking the tracks came across a large box lying carelessly in the snow, and my Grandfather's name was on it. It was too heavy for him alone to carry, so he ran all the way to my grandparents' house, spreading news of the package along the way. By the time my mother's family received word of it, the whole town was buzzing with excitement. The men ran down to the track with my Grandfather to retrieve the package, while the women and children gathered in my Grandmother's kitchen. My Grandmother baked a yellow cake of sorts, substituting corn meal for flour, then drizzled sugar water with orange flavoring over the top for frosting, and my mother recalls that it was good.

Finally, the moment arrived. The men were jovial and the children breathless with excitement as each coveted item was lifted from the box with care. There were new winter coats for each of the children, and boots and shoes. Blue jeans for Grandpa and the boys. Also, each boy received a pocketknife and a "Lindy" cap (like the one worn by Charles Lindbergh during his Trans-Atlantic flight) and new dresses for the girls. As a special surprise Grandpa had ordered a blue dress for my Grandmother with a small white flower print, and an "Evening in Paris" cologne set.

Good times were scarce in those days, and the neighbors were reluctant to leave after the festivities. But finally, the last bite of cake was eaten, and the last goodbye said. For many years after, the townspeople referred to this event as "The Grand Opening."

And so...lately I've been thinking of my grandparents and the heritage they've given me. Twelve generations we can go back on my grandmother's side...all of them crying out never to be forgotten. As long as we can write or speak, the old stories will be told. These are my roots, deep- as an old tree...deeper than the abandoned coal mines of West Virginia...and I wanted to share it with you.

Nancy
1995

NANCY INGRID HURD

FIG. 2 – MY FAMILY TREE
(on my maternal Grandmothers side)

The Carpenters can trace back twelve generations....

1. Nathaniel Carpenter

2. Joseph Cole Carpenter (killed by Mingo & Delaware Indians)

3. William Carpenter (killed by Shawnee)

4. Jeremiah Carpenter (abducted by Shawnee from age 9-18. Later married a Shawnee woman)

5. Solomon Carpenter (son of Jeremiah & Shawnee wife)

6. William ("Squirrely Bill") Carpenter (great outdoorsman, storyteller, fiddler)

7. Jehu Carpenter

8. Eliza Carpenter (my grandmother)

9. Patricia Nine Hurd (my mother)

10. Nancy Ingrid Hurd Sampson (moi)

11. Rebecca Rush Klein-Neil Andrew Rush (my children)

12. Owen Alexander Klein (Rebecca and Daniel's son) and Cora Adalyn Rush (Neil & Stephanie's daughter)

*Obviously, my ancestors had the bad habit of settling on Native American land.

NANCY INGRID HURD

My Grandparents, Walter and Eliza Nine

My Grandmother, Eliza Carpenter Nine

To David, My Brother

In distant memory is the seedling oak
That sprouted before I was born.
He would push a chair beside my crib
And help me climb out each morn.
His hands were warm and bigger than mine;
Only bigger than sixteen months difference in time;
And our time was the sun, the flowers, and wind,
And the echo of nursey rhyme.
His skin had the hue of the Indian in him
Traced back to that primeval wood
When a grandmother thrice or four times removed
Was entrapped, so they say, as a slave-
Or willingly wooed by a brave,
Whose nomadic mind 'neath a crimson moon
Was subdued to wed and conceive
And leave his mark on the first one I knew
Other than my mother-the child of the wild-
My brother

With Love,
from Pat

(Written by my mother for her oldest bother.)

NANCY INGRID HURD

REMEMBERING GRANDMA

April 9th, 1990

My grandmother, Eliza Ellen Carpenter Nine, died yesterday. During an afternoon nap she slipped quietly away. Her family surrounded her, weeping their last goodbyes, until the ambulance arrived to take her to West Virginia University Hospital, where she had donated her body for medical research. Even in death, her purpose was to continue giving, just as she had so richly given during her lifetime.

My grandfather, Walter Irvin Nine, to whom she had been married for sixty-three years, gently patted her hand as they carried her away, then sadly watched from the window as she went down Church Street for the last time. Modestly, she did not want to be memorialized-but please, let me tell you about my grandmother.

As children our trips to Grandma's house were referred to as "going down home." How we looked forward to those visits! Some of my earliest and fondest memories are of the comfort and security felt there by the love showered upon us by aunts, uncles and grandparents. I remember soft summer nights, my sister and I spinning and swaying in the darkness of her front porch, Grandma's long, frilly nightgowns which she allowed us to wear, sweeping around our small, bare feet...the sweet smell of honeysuckles thick in the air where they climbed profusely up her trellises.

I remember also the ever-present "little bit of foolishness" beneath the domed lid of her cake plate and the spoonfuls of rich frosting left intentionally in mixing bowls for her grandkids to lick clean and wonderful light loaves of homemade bread rising in the warmth of her kitchen. But most importantly, I remember her being there-for every recital, graduation, marriage, birth-she was always there. Disappointed that her own children had not been blessed with

13

doting grandmothers, she decided while still a young woman that when she had grandchildren, she would excel in being loving, caring and helpful. In my heart I felt and feel that she was the best. I'm sure that all her many descendants, grandchildren and great grandchildren would agree!

Problems seemed few and surmountable in Grandma's presence. She helped us laugh our cares away, (she was gifted with a rare sense of humor), or eat them away, (she was a wonderful cook). But I'm sure she will be remembered foremost for her sense of humor. Her wit was quick. Her fascinating stories gave us hours of listening pleasure, challenging our imaginations with tales, both comical and adventurous, of places and people she had known, including her Braxton County, West Virginia relatives, many of them also story tellers, who like Grandma were from pioneer stock. She was also gifted in her ability to make us feel good about ourselves; simply because she believed that we were good and worthy and beautiful.

Grandma loved flowers. Through the borders of her vast garden narrowed as she aged, they flourished under her loving care. Years ago, I visited a place where Grandma had lived as a young wife and mother. The house was no longer standing, having burnt to the ground years before, but perennials she had planted were still blooming in the yard. I picked a bouquet and took them to her. Grandma never showed her feelings freely, but tears filled her eyes. "Thank you, Honey," she said quietly as she arranged them in a vase. She had always felt an attachment to that old farm, perhaps because her own children had been babies there. Perhaps because one of those babies, little Joey, lay buried in the land beyond the house.

Grandma was a handsome woman, but never accepted compliments gracefully. When commended on how nice she looked in a new outfit, she would always lament that it had "looked good on the hanger."

Grandma...I envision her now as she was then, opening her bedroom door, ready to step out for her weekly shopping trip to Fairmont, stylishly dressed with lipstick, rouge and jewelry and her hair rolled meticulously into a French twist, the smells of hairspray and cologne enveloping her. The years fade away and I am a child again, standing in awe before this amazing woman who could go from knee-deep in a blackberry patch to sheer elegance so quickly. "Grandma," I exclaim, "you're beautiful!" (Grandma you WERE beautiful). And in an instant, I hear that old humor snapping back at me through the years. "Yes", she says, "I am beautiful-if you look real fast".

Grandma is gone now, but in my mind and heart she is still coaxing her abundant garden to grow, tidying up the old house on Church Street as she waits for Grandpa to come home from the mines; cooking delicious meals and molding loaves of fresh, white bread in her capable hands, just as she shaped, molded and enriched all of our lives.

She will forever be "down home" in my memory.

With Love, Nancy

NANCY INGRID HURD

The following two stories were told by my grandfather, Walter I. Nine in his later years to his daughter and my mother, Patricia Nine Hurd. Grandpa passed away on February 9th, 2001 at the age of ninety-four.

UNCLE LUTE & THE KLAN

(Stories told by Dad - #9)
By Patricia Nine Hurd

Yes, the smartest thing I ever did was buy this reading machine."

I had just walked in the back door and found Dad sitting at the desk in the corner of the living room sliding the lower tray back and forth which held his reading material, as he leaned forward scanning the lighted screen where the print was projected and magnified, bringing each word to life.

"I know I spent a lot of money on this," he continued. "But I had no choice. I hope you're wearing your sunglasses and eating your greens. Macular degeneration is a wicked thing."

"Now that you've read all the books in your library," I observed. "I see you've started on the encyclopedias."

"I'm reading about the Ku Klux Clan," he answered. "I didn't realize it had been around for such a long time. It says here it was founded in 1866 right after the Civil War. At first it was a social group for war veterans, but then it got out of hand and began to terrorize former slaves. And it's been terrorizing ever since. And all along I had thought it started in the early 1900's when I was a kid. Probably because that was the first I'd ever heard of it."

Dad left his reading machine and slowly made his way to his rocking chair in the kitchen.

"I just had lunch," he told me, "but there's some oyster stew on the stove. Get a bowl out of the cabinet and help yourself. It's good, even if I did make it." He smiled as he settled into his rocker and I settled at the kitchen table with lunch before me and the hope of hearing more from Dad about the Klan.

"How old were you when you first knew about it?" I asked him.

"Probably around six. That would have been 1912. I had heard there was a group of men who were burning crosses. I didn't know many of the details. My parents always talked about it in hushed tones when we kids were around. But I did hear that they sent some sort of warning letter to our local jeweler. He was Jewish. I forget his name; it was something or other 'stein.'

"Anyway, we were sitting at the breakfast table one morning. It was a Saturday I remember, because my Dad was home. I could tell he was agitated about something. He was frowning and kept staring off into space and fidgeting with his coffee spoon. That was unusual for Dad. He was a calm sort, not easily ruffled. Suddenly he turned to me and said, 'Walter, would you like to go to a parade?'

"Well, I could feel myself getting all excited. We didn't get much entertainment then, not like kids today. Having something as thrilling as that sprung on me, was almost more than I could handle. Immediately through, my mother told him in no uncertain terms that he was not to go. But Dad stood his ground and insisted. He told Mom he had been hearing tales and had to find out for himself."

Dad further related how excited he was that afternoon to be standing on the sidewalk of Main Street, Oakland, with his father and numerous other town and country folks who had heard about the big event. Dad told me they kept waiting to hear the sound of a band in the distance, but instead of horns, as one would expect, what they did hear was the measured boom-boom of a large brass drum that kept getting louder as it drew close.

"I kept craning my neck in the direction of all that noise," Dad continued. "I expected to see men in uniforms with braid and brass buttons, but here came this group of people, about fifty of them or more, all wearing white sheets and pointed white hoods with eye holes cut in them. They were marching probably four abreast. That drum kept beating and they kept coming. I thought they were a bunch of ghosts! I let go of Dad's hand and latched on thigh to the tail of his jacket. Then above the drum beat I heard Dad say, 'Just as I expected!'"

"I just looked up and saw this large built man with a limp approaching, white sheet and all. As he got closer to Dad and me, he turned his head just slightly in our direction. He kept his arm straight down, but he gave us a little sideway wave with his fingers as he marched by. Suddenly at the top of his voice, your grandfather let out an obscenity directed at this man that was easily heard above all that clang and clamor. That was the first and last time I'd heard my father use such language.

He then grabbed my hand and turned abruptly and headed for home. He was taking such strides I could hardly keep up with him. After a while he slowed down and placed his hand on my shoulder and asked me if I know who that man was. I told him I did. He stooped over till he was eye level with me, I've never forgotten what he said. 'Don't ever be proud of your Uncle Lute,' he told me."

For a few moments Dad sat quietly, deep in thought, his mind on an incident that had happened decades in the past. At length he related that he did not remember the matter ever being discussed again in the family; at least not openly. But, however, from that day on his father and his Uncle Luther were no longer on speaking terms.

"You mean those two brothers never spoke to each other again?" I asked him.

"No, not as far as I know," he replied. "We never visited them. They never visited us."

"There's something rather sad about that," I told him.

"What makes me sad," he answered, "is the fact that one group of bigoted people can set themselves up as being superior and causing trouble for other people. My father taught me a valuable lesson at age six and it has stuck with me all these years to age ninety."

We sat quietly in Dad's cozy kitchen, listening to the creak of his rocking chair. I then reminded him that when I was quite young, but in a far less dramatic way, by his example and guidance, he had taught me the same lesson.

THE BAPTISM OF NORIE SNIDEBROOK

(Stories told by Dad - #2)
By Patricia Nine Hurd

Everywhere she went she had to make a big splash! Always drawing attention to herself. I'm sure glad your mother wasn't like that!" Dad hesitated for a moment as a look of pride crossed his face. "Your mother was a lady. I was always grateful for that!"

"I assume Norie Snidebrook wasn't a lady. What was she like? Was she attractive?" I asked him.

"No! And that's another thing I couldn't understand. Why would a fat, homely woman want to be the center of attention? You'd think she would have wanted to hide. She always talked loud! You could hear her a mile away~! She walked fast; sort of bounced along in a waddling way. Most women wore their hair long then but swept it up on top of their heads with fancy combs and doodads. But not Norie! Hers hung down her back and switched from side to side like a horse's tail. You almost expected to see burrs in it."

This had the making of one of Dad's amusing stories from the past, so I questioned him further regarding the notorious Norie.

"She was youngish," Dad continued. "Had five or six small children who always trailed behind her. The oldest, a girl about ten or so always carried the baby. When her husband was home, he'd carry the baby and trail behind her with the kids. He was a logger: worked away most of the time; a small built man. He never had much to say, which stood to reason.

"When they'd come to a social gathering Norie would always draw attention to her contribution, she'd go on and on about how the icing on her cake cost almost a dollar. But she wasn't going to spare any expense. 'You know me,' she'd say.

"When they'd arrive at church on Sunday mornings, even if they were late, which they often were, she'd make a big to do about finding seats for all the family and thought nothing of asking people to 'move over just one'. This always caused a disturbance and whoever was leading the meeting would stop talking until all the Snidebrooks were settled in."

"I was around eleven at the time," Dad continued, "and attended the Knob Hill School. One cold, frosty morning we had just started our first lesson when we heard a big commotion outside the building-a lot of people talking, and above it all was Norie Snidebrooks's loudmouth. Miss Bertha, our teacher rolled her eyes, heaved a big sigh and went to investigate."

Dad further stated that when she returned, she had an almost smirking smile on her face, which she was trying hard to conceal from her pupils. It seemed that during the night Mrs. Snidebrook had some sort of revelation and wanted to be baptized immediately. It couldn't wait! The church was three quarters of a mile down the road, but it always used the pond in the turn of the creek by the school for baptisms, which ordinarily took place during the spring or summer.

Since Norie had been eager to inform as many people as possible of her divine experience, it had aroused the curiosity of many of the townsfolk, who had hurried to the site of the ceremony, led by old Preacher Mossbacher, who had been jerked away from his breakfast table by the insistent zealot. The purpose of his conference with Miss Bertha, was to inform her of the occasion since it was customary to turn school out for all important events.

Dad said when he walked outside into the cold morning air and his nostrils stuck together with every breath, he wasn't so concerned about Norie; who was wearing some sort of long, white flowing thing that looked like a flannel nightgown, and who was all fired up and shouting "Praise the Lord"; as he was about the old preacher who was anxiously eying the layers of ice on the pond.

"I knew they were going to need some depth," Dad asserted. "Norie Snidebrook was a big woman! Some of us older boys broke the ice by throwing stones into the creek as far out as they needed to go. Before the old parson dunked her under, he gave the shortest prayer I ever heard. He had some difficulty pulling her back up and at one point almost went under with her.

But finally, the deed was done, and she came running from the water like a charging buffalo. Several of the women present met her at the bank's edge with blankets which they wrapped around her as they hurried her off to the waiting horse buggy. The old preacher, who was wet to his waist and shaking like an aspen leaf, barely made it to the shore, and no one offered him a blanket."

As the narrative continued Dad related that during the course of the day, Miss Bertha excused herself several times and practically ran to the cloak room, where muffled crying-or was it laughing-could be heard by those who were sitting in the back of the room, he being one of them. "Each time she emerged," Dad said, "she would wipe the tears from her eyes and say, 'baptisms are so emotional.' But we all noticed she still had that little, smirky grin on her face."

Dad further stated that the fame of Norie's sudden baptism spread far and wide. Some of the honest-hearted area folks felt indignant and remarked that she had accomplished her purpose. As usual, she wanted to make a big splash, which literally, she did! But a few of the old die-hard fanatics felt it was a true sign from heaven and that all folks would do well to follow Mrs.
Snidebrook's example.

"Then there was another line of thought regarding Norie's cleansing from sin," Dad concluded. "And that was the one that Mom said was whispered among the ladies at the quilting bee. Mr. Snidebrook worked away; and the area was teeming with lumberjacks, oil and gas men and railroad workers. Some folks were of the opinion that during the previous night of her baptism, Norie Snidebrook had committed some grave, serious sin."

"And what did you think?" I asked him.

"I never did believe that," he replied firmly.

"Dad," I said, "how kind of you to give Norie the benefit of the doubt."

"Norie?" he exclaimed. "Not Norie" I gave those workmen the benefit of the doubt!"

my life...

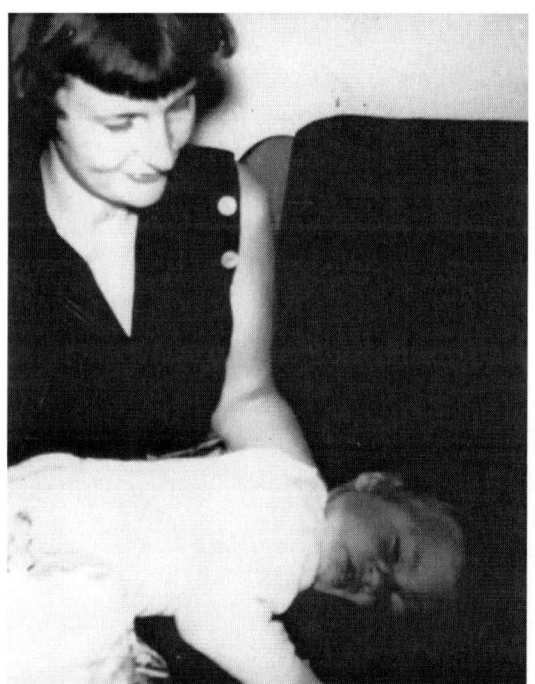

My Mother & Me

"Sweet and low,
Sweet and low,
Wind of the Western Sea;
Low, low, breathe and blow,
Over the rolling waters we go,
Come from the dying morn
Sweet and low...
Blow him again to me,
Blow him again to me,
While my little one...
While my pretty one sleeps."

Lullaby

MY ARRIVAL

In the afternoon of June 28th, 1955, I was born. My mother said it was an incredibly easy birth. In fact, it was this very ease of passage that could have been problematic. Had my mother not been bold and assertive with the attending nurses.

The doctor had checked Mom early in the afternoon and informed her that delivery was at best, several hours away, and that he was going to go home and take a nap.

Immediately after his departure, Mom went into hard labor...she called out to the nurse, "my baby is coming!" "No", the nurse answered casually, "the doctor said you have hours to go." "This baby is coming!" my mother demanded. Undaunted, the nurse insisted that she was mistaken.

Mom then threw off the covers and spread her legs apart.

"Oh my God!" the nurse screamed and yelled for other nurses to come, since the doctor was no longer around, and I was "crowning".

As one nurse wheeled Mom to the delivery room screaming, "This baby is coming! Don't bother to scrub!" Another nurse ran beside the cart squeezing Mom's legs together. "Stop that!" Mom demanded "you will damage its head! You let this baby come!"

So, the nurse did, and so did I, before reaching the delivery room, with two nurses and my mother to welcome me into the world.

"It was like a knife through butter," Mom recalls. "I felt absolutely no pain. You just came out."

I wish all my life had been so easy! The place was the Fairmont General Hospital, Fairmont, West Virginia. The same hospital where my father was born.

... So ...where was my Father on that momentous day, you may wonder....

At this writing I am 63 years old. Tonight, I am searching through Dad's 337-page memoir trying to find something about his impression of my birth. It is a rare privilege to have a written account by one's parent documenting their entry into this world. My Father's memoirs are filled with his life as a naval officer, diligently scrambling up the ladder, constantly striving to increase rank. I am mentioned almost as an afterthought, amid page after page of military affairs.

That being said, I am grateful for this written documentation of his life and was inspired by him to do the same for my children, only with more emphasis on family and relationships. Because when the tide of our life rolls away, what matters most will not be our secular accomplishments, or how many letters accumulated behind our name.... but how much value was placed on those people who were put in front of us to love. How much did we truly love? Everything else is "vanity and striving after the wind" ...Everything, and everyone turns to dust. Like my father's memoirs yellowing in a box in the bottom of my closet.

Here are his memories of my arrival...or more accurately, his arrival into my life...

"In June (1955) we were finished with our three-month training and shake down period and headed back to the U.S. On June 29 I got a radio message via the ship communication center that Pat had a baby girl the day before and that everything was alright. I asked for, and was granted a 5-day leave, to commence the day we arrived in New York.

I was on pins and needles all the way back from Cuba, for I knew nothing more than the terse message conveyed by telegram. I didn't know the baby's name or anything about it. The ship stopped at Norfolk on the way up, so I left and headed for home.

It was dawn when I arrived; not a soul was stirring anywhere. I came back to a house I had never lived in, but where my family now was, fast asleep and not aware that I was home. Pat, Joey, Greta and the baby I had never seen. It was very early, the morning gray and cool. I looked at the little house from down the road and imagined them up there asleep in their beds and baby cribs.

I went to the door and lightly knocked. It opened immediately; Pat was in my arms before I realized she was there. I had been wrong about her sleeping. She had been awake and waiting for me. She was beautiful!

I looked in the little room where the children all slept. There was Joey in his new bed, and Greta and Nancy each in a crib. It seemed strange looking at Nancy for the first time; she was just a few weeks old but had smooth complexion and black hair. She was a pretty baby and there was no way of knowing then that soon her hair would turn completely white." ...

So, there it is. My Father spent 3 days with us before being shipped off to the far corners of the world for the best part of a year, I saw him for a few days at 9 months old, then not again until I was nearly two.

I still remember the latter home coming. He held me for a long time and felt like a stranger to me... then sat me down on the floor and placed a wind up white furry kitty in front of me...I still remember how fascinated I was by all the gold on his uniform.

I love this man dearly.

But quite naturally, was never attached to him as I have been to my mother.

Even so:

> "I thank you for your kindness and the times when you got tough / And Papa, I don't think I said, 'I love you' near enough."

Dan Fogelberg
(from Leader of the Band)

Pat Hurd & her children in 1957, somewhere in the Rockies.

A NIGHT IN THE STARS

The summer of 1957, our family took the long, arduous journey from San Diego, California, where Dad had been on active duty for two years, back to our home state of West Virginia. Mostly we camped along the way. Dad, raising our Army green canvas tent every night, while Mom cooked dinner over a small gas grill and bathed her children in a basin beneath a canopy of trees.

There were six of us in all...Mom, Dad, my older siblings Joe and Greta, myself and our canine companion...a huge, slightly out of control Newfoundland, named Neptune.

I was only two years old at the time, but still have a few fond memories of this trek across the country.

One night, exhausted from the rigors of the journey, Dad decided to splurge for a night in a little Norman Bates style motel, the type which was so popular and plentiful in the 1950's. I remember a bath...the first one in days...and the sound of my own muffled screams, ears submerged in the sudsy water, as Mom rinsed shampoo from my hair. On went my "onesies", and suddenly I was whisked out of the motel room door, and onto a blanket in the yard, where Dad, Joe and Greta were lying, looking up at the stars.

Instantly the trauma of my recent shampoo vanished, as I lay mesmerized by the vast and beautiful universe above me. I had never noticed the night sky before...and the sound of Dad's quiet voice explaining mysteries to my brother and sister, who were old enough to understand. Orion's belt, red Venus, the Big and Little Dippers.

As I lay feeling contentment and awe, I knew there was something far grander than this little family lying on a blanket in the yard of an old motel, taking a magic carpet ride across the sky. Something more was out there in that big, wide, unbelievable expanse...and I would grope for the meaning of it one day. I have been searching for it all my life.

But on this night, it was enough to lie there yawing against my father's back...his softly droning voice...the sky overhead...my mother unpacking a suitcase through the light of an open door...and the stars going out, one...by one...by one...

Nancy, September 2017

"...We lived on a street
where the tall elm shade
was as green as the grass
and as cool as a blade
that you held in your teeth
as we lay on our backs
staring up at the blue
and the blue stared back

I used to believe we were
just like those trees
we'd grow just as tall and as
proud as we pleased
with our feet on the ground
and our arms in the breeze
under a sheltering sky

Twirl me about and twirl me around
let me grow dizzy and fall to the ground
and when I look up at you looking down
say it was only a dream..."

Mary Chapin Carpenter

NANCY INGRID HURD

WINTER MEMORY

I am taken back in time to the winter of 1959. It is the middle of the night and I am four years old. I stray to the window at the top of the stairs in the old Victorian house where we live in Dennison, Ohio.

Snow is falling and I am magnetized. It is no ordinary snow. It is soft and billowy, and unusually heavy...like an enormous feather pillow has burst in half time over our town. It sparkles like gems under the streetlight.

Suddenly there are arms around me and I am lifted to my father's knee as he kneels in the darkness...and he is talking to me...soft as the gently falling snow...about how it's late and I should be sleeping...and about how beautiful it is outside, and how lucky we are to be safe and warm inside on such a night...and I feel safe and warm.

Not because of the four walls surrounding us, but because of this man whose arms encircle me...and the sound of his quiet voice as we share this precious moment in our lives...which has come to be my favorite winter memory.

Nancy
Blowing Rock, NC

NANCY INGRID HURD

My Mother circa 1940s

Me & my mother 2004

MOM

We were children of the sixties. The "Cold War" was looming, the "Bay of Pigs" had just occurred, Viet Nam was gathering momentum and the Second World War still breathing down our backs. Times were turbulent and uncertain, and she was afraid for her children. We all felt her concern, but as an especially sensitive child, I did perhaps more than the others.

Unable to relate to adult fears, I wrapped my mind around the images created by an anxious six-year-old...cats ready to pounce on my feet as I jumped into bed at night...clouds falling from the sky, (the idea was suffocating!).

Thunderstorms, and as soon as I could grasp, (and I grasped it early), the meaning of death...that these vibrant, pulsating bodies and minds full of plans and ideas could just disappear into that all-encompassing darkness...I was horrified! (I am still horrified.)

Since I was such an insecure child, very early in life my mother became my security. With a comforting word she could banish every fear.

Mom worked hard for her family. We children were always scrubbed as shiny as her "Johnson's" waxed floors. Dad was a schoolteacher and his white, starched shirts could have stood alone. Meals were not elaborate, but good and healthy by 1950's standards. Dr Spock was her guidebook, seeing us through all our childhood illnesses.

I remember how she would sit up all night long when one of her babies had the croup, making a steam tent around the rocking chair. I remember how she rocked me for hours when I was six years old and had the measles. It was so comforting to lie against her shoulder and hear her sing all the old lullabies...songs her mother had sung to her...and her mother before that...one about twenty froggies going to school, "down beside a rushy pool, twenty little coasts of green, twenty vests all white and clean." Songs I now sing to my grandchildren.

She was scrupulous about our clothes and hair, and our manners when in the company of adults, were to be impeccable. This was enforced. My father and brothers never sat down to the dinner table if mother and sisters were still standing. My brothers always removed their hats in the presence of ladies. We were given lessons in common courtesy, (not so common anymore!) and were quickly corrected if we stepped out of line. She spanked freely...and loved lavishly.

My mother...she is old now, living in that cozy two story house in Oak Forest, Pennsylvania...the one she purchased and remodeled almost single handedly. She fills her days with books, letter writing and old movies. She feeds birds and has beautiful flowers in the Summertime.

I call her frequently, and write, but worry about her living alone and so far away. "Do you ever get depressed?" I asked recently. "Why, no!" she said, "I don't let my head get into a fog! I was depressed for a while at age eighteen, but I shook it off and didn't allow myself to go there again." Unimaginable resilience.

I admire her strength and depend on it, relying on her folk wisdom, encouragement, and sage advice. I always knew, if called upon to do so, she would crawl through fire for me.

No one else in life will love you like that, and when your mother goes, you have lost your best friend. As John F. Kennedy Jr. said when Jackie passed away, "No matter how old you are, when your mother dies, you are an orphan."

When she is gone, I will draw on that ever flowing well of emotional nourishment and maternal love for the rest of my days...for she gave enough to last a lifetime. And I will never say goodbye. Not to her...not ever.

ROCK ME TO SLEEP

Come let your brown hair
Just lighted with gold
Fall on your shoulders again
As of old.
Let it drop over my
Forehead tonight,
Shading my faint eyes
Away from the light...
For with its sunny edged
Shadows once more
Haply will throng the sweet
Visions of yore
Lovingly, softly, its bright
Billows sweep...
Rock me to sleep mother,
Rock me to sleep

Mother, sweet mother
The years have been long
Since I last listened
Your lullaby song
...sing them, and unto my soul
It shall seem
Womanhood's years have been
Only a dream.
Clasped to your heart
In a loving embrace,
With your light lashes
Just sweeping my face,
Never thereafter
To wake, or to weep...
Rock me to sleep mother,
Rock me to sleep!

Elizabeth Akers Allen

NANCY INGRID HURD

**Mom's children in more recent years:
Jon, Walter, Nancy, Greta & Joe**

Family 1965

THE AUTUMN OF INALOU MALLONE

It was the fall of 1961 when Inalou Mallone moved to our town. We were six years old at the time and attended Mrs. James' first grade glass in an old brick schoolhouse in the little town of Dennison, Ohio.

Inalou was small...much smaller than I. In fact, she was the smallest child in class...and she was dirty...and she smelled badly. Her clothes were worn thin and her chronically uncombed hair in a tangle. Her fingernails were filthy and in desperate need of trimming. All of these were offenses I might easily have overlooked had she just kept her distance. But she did not...so I could not.

I don't know where Inalou came from, and later, after she was taken away, I often wondered where she had gone. I am fifty-two-year-old now...and sometimes I still wonder.

She sat silently in her assigned seat each day, never raising her hand and seldom raising her head. When noon time rolled around the rest of us raced for our lunch boxes on the shelf in the cloak room, then gathered in circles on the floor for childish chatter over milk and peanut butter.

But Inalou sat alone at her desk with hands folded in front of her. She had no lunch and we didn't care. Mrs. James saw the plight of this little girl and kindly started bringing an extra sandwich for her. But she still ate alone...and we still didn't care.

We were middle class "baby boomer" children in the early sixties and Inalou was an intruder. She wasn't like the rest of us. She wasn't like me...and I didn't want her in my world.

Ours was the largest yard in the neighborhood, and on those warm autumn evenings every child in town converged upon it for breathless games of tag or hide-and-seek. One evening as my turn came around for "Red Rover"; I looked down our tree-lined street and saw Inalou walking slowly toward my house. Her head was down, and she didn't even glance our way...and of course none of us invited her to play.

Later, when my mother called us in for dinner, imagine my surprise when there was Inalou with head down as usual, sitting at our supper table. No one had warned me that this little interloper was to be our dinner guest...and she ate like a lumberjack.

I realized in later years that this child, trying desperately to get her needs met, had been drawn almost intuitively to our home and my mother...for after that first meal, she appeared on our doorstep every evening...half frightened, unkempt, wide-eyed and alone. Rain or shine, she was always there.

Through neighborhood gossip my mother learned that Inalou had no father and that her mother was an alcoholic. They lived in a big, old, barren rental house on the edge of town with no electricity or running water. Since there was scarcely any furniture, Inalou slept on a blanket on the floor.

(The fact is, she was pitifully ignored, neglected and possibly even physically abused during a time when there were few laws in place to protect such children.)

But she had instinctively sought out and found refuge and comfort in my mother...my mother! I didn't mind sharing Mom with my siblings, since that is the normal way of things and cannot be helped...but oh, how I hated sharing her with this little stranger!

One evening after my bath I came downstairs to find Mom and Inalou baking Toll House cookies together. They laughed as my mother taught her the magic of dunking warm chocolate chip cookies into a glass of milk. It was the first time I had ever seen the girl smile.

Every evening after that, my mother took on some new project concerning this semi-orphaned child. She made her bathe, gave her a toothbrush, and after a good shampoo, cut her hair into a stylish "bob". Then she cleaned and trimmed those filthy nails.

I felt jealousy at seeing them sitting together on the couch while Mom painted her nails with clear polish. But the greatest indignity of all came when Inalou became the recipient of all my hand-me-downs. She had taken my mother, and now she was taking my clothes. It was too much to bear.

But even I could see how the child was blossoming. Where she once sat stark and silent in class, she now began raising her manicured little hand when the teacher asked questions. She also began reading aloud in our reading circle...and she read well! Her once pale cheeks were turning rosy pink, her body plumping beneath my beloved old dresses, her hair shining, her eyes bright... and she began to play, and talk, and laugh.

I just wanted her quiet gain...I just wanted her gone.

Each evening after dinner Mom would ask Inalou to sleep over. Her answer was always the same, her disappointment obvious. She could not stay. So, it became the job of my older sister and me to walk her home. She would stop by the church on the corner at the end of her street and tell us to go back...she could walk the rest of the way alone.

I knew Inalou was ashamed of where she lived. But I could see in the distance the big old house...more of a barn really...looking all dark and lonesome out of the windows. I could picture her mother lying intoxicated in the gloomy solitude as Inalou crept quietly past on her way to the floor/bed in the corner.

One day Inalou didn't show up for school. Mrs. James was concerned. But when she missed the next day and the next...my mother, with a baby on her hip, half walked and half ran all the way to Inalou's house and found, just as she had feared, that it was empty.

She looked through the windows for some sign of life but saw nothing to indicate that the previous occupants planned to return. There were a few bags of garbage, some empty liquor bottles, and on the floor in a corner, a rumpled pillow and blanket where someone had slept.

My bedroom in those days was across the hall from my parents. That night in the darkness I could hear my Mom crying and my father's voice...steady and comforting. I worried that my mean spiritedness had caused Inalou to go away and create this great sadness in my mother. The following day Dad made some inquires, but to no avail...we never saw her again.

And so, the years have passed. Often, I have wondered if Inalou survived her turbulent childhood. Did a stable foster family find her? Did loving relatives rescue her? Did she ever have pink wallpaper or a favorite doll? Did she marry and have children of her own to love and protect as she had not been? Did she miss my mother?

My mother...that's who this story is about. This is in celebration of that lady who with five children of her own, and two still in diapers, took in a strange child to nourish and nurture simply because no one else would... she never mentioned Inalou again. But I know she never forgot the sad little girl whose life she most assuredly changed forever.

My mother did that...my mother...whose rare example chiseled out some important life lessons for me...lessons in compassion and kindness extended to others, even when it is hard or inconvenient...and how fragile are the ties binding we humans together on this planet. So we must always reach out...reach out...a little here, a little there, to strengthen the delicate cord of humanity we all cling to.

These lessons I learned all those years ago in the Autumn of Inalou Mallone.

Nancy 2007

SIFTING THROUGH THE ASHES

Park Elementary School, Dennison, Ohio

KELLEY JANE

Children could roam the village of Dennison, Ohio freely and alone in 1961, without much trepidation.

I remember one evening sitting wide-eyed in the kitchen, as my mother in the way of a lesson, related to me how a child in New York City had spoken to a stranger and been abducted right out of her yard.

But New York City was far away and crimes against children almost unheard of in those days.

So, it was not unusual one Sunday morning as my mother stood on the sidewalk in front of our house chatting pleasantly with an elderly neighbor, to see five-year-old Kelley Jane approaching. She was all decked out in a frilly dress, stand out petticoats, patent leather shoes and Shirley Temple curls. Kelley had been to Sunday school, left before church services, and stopped by "Coonies" grocer on her way home to spend her collection plate money on a bag of penny candy.

"You look beautiful this morning, Kelley Jane!", my mother remarked as Kelley came closer. "Have you been to Sunday school?" "Yep," Kelley answered with that signature gleam in her eye..."and I spent all my collection plate money on candy."

"Why, Kelley Jane!" our neighbor lady said reproachfully..." don't you know that was GOD'S money?"

"Well," Kelley Jane grinned, with red dye from a 'jaw breaker' around her sticky mouth... "God didn't get it today."

NANCY INGRID HURD

THE WONDER YEARS

In 1962 we left our beloved Victorian home on Miller Avenue, in Dennison, Ohio, where we had lived in an "Ozzie and Harriet" type post war bliss for nearly five years.

Dad had taken a teaching position at nearby Urichsville High School after our sojourn from San Diego to West Virginia...unexpected events had landed us in Ohio...and Mom stayed home, as was the custom for mothers of that era...to care for her ever-growing family.

We had wonderful neighbors and children living up and down our brick paved, tree lined street. My days were filled with play and magical adventure.

I see them still...the faces of my early childhood friends...

Christine, an older girl and matriarch of our little circle.

Debbie, the maternal one who always treated me with a bossy loving-ness.

Lyla, my best friend and classmate once I was old enough to go to school.

Nanette, who never tired of playing "horses" ...

Georgie and Andy, Lyla's older brothers. I remember throwing a rock at Georgie's head one time, just to see if "big boys cry."

I remember being dragged into the house and punished by my mother.

I felt sorry for Georgie and very ashamed of myself. He told me it hurt his feelings more than his head. They were a Polish family who had escaped the Holocaust to find love and acceptance in our little community.

Then there were Christine's siblings, Molly Kay the baby and Timmy who loved every creeping and crawling thing, had a crush on my sister and died many years later as a true adventurer in the Alaskan wilderness.

...And of course, there was Kelley Jane, child of my heart who could always make me laugh. We have remained friends to this day.

Our departure from this beautiful chapter in our lives occurred when Dad decided to move back to West Virginia to work on his master's degree at W.V. University...where grandparents lived nearby and could give support as we transitioned.

It was a momentous shock to our family. I have never been happier than during our Dennison "wonder years" and have missed it all my life.

And we were missed, too. Kelley Jane told me many years later after reconnecting on Facebook, that the day our old station wagon drove down Miller Avenue for the last time, she sat on the bottom step of our front porch and cried until her mother came and carried her home.

These happy early years were like a mist that came up from the ground, nurturing me in ways that many children never get to experience. But it all disappeared in the scorching noon day sun.

I had no choice but to move on.

THE GRANT TOWN YEARS

In 1964 Dad hired Joe, Greta, and me to clean "Ballah Chapel Church" in Grant Town, WV where he served as superintendent. We worked on Saturday evenings for 2 or 3 hours and were paid fifty cents an hour.

I truly hated that job. But we, and especially Greta, saved our money and bought a spirited black, brown and white spotted pony and after a family meeting, settled on naming him "Poncho" ...what a handful he was! But Greta loved him dearly, and became a very good rider, despite his frequent attempts to throw her off and trample her. I was terrified of hm! As well I should have been, Poncho hated me.

One evening as we were starting our work at the church, our old Parson, Marvin Miller, who cried during his emotional sermons, (my Grandmother said he put pepper in his handkerchiefs), came over from the rectory to speak with Dad about something. He stared down at us kids through his beady little eyes and said, as he crushed a filter less cigarette butt beneath his shoe, "someone," then raised his eyes toward heaven... "is watching over you children all the time. He loves you and sees everything you do."

Well...I already knew this and lived in dread of it. It seemed to me that Santa...terrifying as he was, only watched me toward the end of the year; whereas God never took a break.

That evening in the church basement I found an ornate bowl filled with water. "Watch this Joe, "I said to my brother, as I proceeded to sprinkle the water on my head. Joe looked at me reproachfully and said, "It's a sin to pretend baptism with holy water."

I was very frightened and spent the rest of the evening praying and singing hymns as I cleaned. It was a real spiritual revival!

That summer we spent long leisurely days playing in Paw Paw Creek or hiking the hill behind Carrie Toothman's house. She was our robust, friendly, gossipy neighbor. I always loved for her to come sit in our kitchen and tell my mother all the latest "news" around town.

I even enjoyed Great Aunt Alma's visits, although I know they made my mother weary. She had seemingly survived every ailment known to man and described each symptom to Mom in the greatest detail. She was a prophetess of doom! We were all bound to get sick and die while in our tender years and she often voiced her concerns over us. Every headache was "meningitis", every bloody nose, leukemia. I believe it would have disappointed her had she lived to see all of us survive childhood.

I love then and love still all the beautiful things of nature and was in constant awe over the magnificent sights, sounds and smells of the lovely, lush countryside surrounding us.

We traveled that year to the southern part of West Virginia to visit my grandmother's sister and brother-in-law, Grace and Lakey Starcher. It was here that I heard a "whip poor will" for the first time.

Uncle Lakey was the overseer of a Girl Scout camp...a beautiful place deep in the woods with a musky lake, where we fished and swam.

There were rustic little cabins where the girls slept, with fireplaces in them. Here we played with our cousin Jackie to our hearts content.

Greta got the flu while we were there and lay in bed, languid with fever. I was frightened and promised God that if he let her live, I would kiss her, something my sister would never tolerate! After making this vow, I realized I had best do it while she was sick and delirious. So, I tiptoed over to the bed and kissed her fast on the forehead. Instantly her eyes opened, and she flashed me a semi-conscious hateful look, as I ran from the room. She recovered, so I know it worked.

That summer our old hound dog, Junior, was hit by a car and died instantly. As with our recently fallen president, John F. Kennedy, I grew fonder of Junior after he was gone. His memory just kept on growing and expanding.

A song was popular that year...a tribute to JFK which when in part..." A young man rode with his head held high, under the Texas sun, and no one guessed that a man so blessed, would perish by the gun..."

While cleaning the church one evening I got to thinking wistfully about old Junior and began to sing-to the tune of the aforementioned Kennedy song, "A young dog walked with his head held high, under the Grant Town star, and no one guessed that a dog so blessed would perish by the car."

The idea quite choked me up, as I ran to the old church piano and began chording it out..."and the heart of the world lays heavy, with the helplessness of tears...for a dog cut down in a little town in the summer of his years..." I even went so far as to sing that "wherever dogs look to freedom, then his soul goes riding on...Lord...his soul goes riding on."

My mother still shivers when she remembers how I buried Junior in a shallow grave, then (unawares) drove a home-made wooden cross right through him. I hung a bouquet of plastic lilacs over the cross and painted on a ceramic plaque..." Junior. He was a good dog."

One morning as I walked to school, I glanced over at his grave and saw that it was all covered over in a layer of white frost with the sun glistening on it.

It really was quite beautiful.

NANCY INGRID HURD

DEATH OF A ROSE

The summer of 1965, I was ten years old. One sunny afternoon my mother informed me that our elderly neighbor, Rose Toothman, had passed away. She was a gentle woman, who smiled at children and greeted us pleasantly when we passed through her yard. She hung fragrant white sheets on the clothesline to dry and planted flowers around her porch. She was a grand-motherly type, and I liked her.

Upon hearing this sad news, I ran to my room and put on one of my Sunday dresses, then went out to the little stone wall at the edge of our yard and picked a bouquet from the wild roses that grew there. I had never seen death before and I was curious...all alone, I climbed the hill to Toothman's house, feeling excitement and dread.

When I entered the parlor, there was Rose lying in a satin-lined coffin in a pink gown. Her white hair was perfectly coiffed in waves around her face making her look younger than she was. She was lovely...and so very still.

I handed my little bouquet to her grateful daughter-in-law, then stood before that casket for a very long time and stared. If I looked long enough, I could imagine that I saw Rose breathing...her breast rising and falling beneath that pretty gown.

I would blink hard and the breathing would stop. It was inconceivable to me that so much effort had obviously been put into making it all look so pretty, when I knew that this was a hideous situation. Rose was gone and soon she would be in the ground rotting like the carcass of an animal on the side of the road. I wanted to cry...but I did not. I spoke awkward words of condolence to the family then started for home.

I felt different that afternoon as I walked down the gravel road and across the railroad track. It became very clear to me what we were all up against, and the inevitability of my own mortality came sweeping over me like a bitter wind.

almost palpable it was...and I could smell it. A sickening sweet smell like the flowers surrounding that coffin in Toothman's parlor. The "way of all flesh" was before me. Like the hound of heaven, it would be yapping and biting at my heels every day of my life until it finally chased me straight into the Abyss. Heavy stuff for a ten-year-old. But I knew something now and could never UN-know it.

As I walked into the cinder block house that was our home, my mother greeted me with hugs. She said that I was the bravest and most considerate girl. And I really listened to her and felt love, appreciation and sorrow for my mother, for I knew that the hound was chasing her too...and everyone I loved.

I wasn't frightened exactly, as I changed back into my play clothes, but I was uneasy. I had swallowed a bitter pill its' true...and one that we all must swallow.

But the sun was shining brightly when I ran out into the yard. My little brothers were shouting for me to come and play. The air was thick as Summertime and the sky bluer than a Robin's egg....and at that moment I knew that life was far greater than any fear of dying...and more precious than I had ever imagined...this I learned all those years ago from the death of Rose Toothman.

Nancy
March 2013

DOG DAYS

I don't know why they call them "Dog Days" or "the dog days of summer" as the old timers used to say, but I think of them as more of a "feeling" than an actual seasonal anomaly.

I remember those long, hot...excruciatingly hot...August days when the air was so close it hovered, like a body closing in on you, invading your boundaries, sweat mingling...bitter...painful...too close for comfort or decency.

I always think of my grandparent's home up on Church Street where aunts and uncles converged in the summertime with cars full of cousins. It was too hot for play or conversation, so we just sat and stared blankly at each other, or lay on the floor to feel the cool tile on our faces. Bored beyond reason...miserable beyond words.

But evening would eventually come and with-it cool air and new life infusion. Grandma would head back to the kitchen after supper to bake a berry cobbler she and my mother had suffered for that afternoon...knee deep in briars in the sweltering sun, risking snake bite, dehydration and tick fever. People used to really work for their food. She would top it with mounds of whipped cream, I mean real whipped cream and it was delicious.

A lightness of spirit settled down on us then as jovial after dinner conversation began. I never tired of hearing the old familiar stories...so rich they rivaled Grandma's cobbler for deliciousness...

And Grandpa...dear old Grandpa...always sitting a little separate from the rest of us, quiet and assured with book in hand, a faint smile on his face...did he even know he provided a stable foundation beneath our chaotic lives?

Now, years later in the solitude of my little apartment with "dog days" descending over my heart like a silent shroud...I remember as though it were yesterday. The smell of honeysuckle thick in the air and laughter bubbling up through the years like a spirit choir singing my life back to me.

What would I give to see my Grandfather again, sitting on the old porch swing? Or catch lightening bugs once more in a jar on a breathless summer night with a yard full of exuberant children? Or taste that blackberry cobbler one more time? ...I guess I would give just about anything.

Nancy
Spring, 2015

The Summer of 1966, after Dad earned his master's degree (two degrees in fact) we moved to Greene County, Pennsylvania, where he accepted a teaching position in foreign languages at Waynesburg College (now University). Waynesburg is a quaint country town in southwestern Pennsylvania. It is here that I spent the remainder of my growing up years.

"...Out of the city
And down to the seaside,
To sun on my shoulders
And wind in my hair,
But sandcastles crumble
And hunger is human
And humans are hungry
For world's they can't share,
My dreams with
The seagulls fly...
Out of reach...
Out of cry"

-Joni Mitchell

THE SUMMER OF CHESAPEAKE BAY

Military life has its perks. The summer of 1966 my father, a commander in the US Navy, was stationed in Norfolk, VA. The rest of the family joined him in August of that eleventh year of my life to spend one glorious month in an apartment facing Chesapeake Bay. It is a summer I will never forget.

I can scarcely describe my first glimpse of the sea. I was magnetized by the powerful endless gray water, stretching to the edge of the horizon...and I ached to be near it! But my father said we must wait until morning. It was late when we arrived, and we had to "settle in".

Dad had already left for the base when we awoke to the sound of sea gulls next morning. Mom, no longer able to contain the excitement of five anxious children, allowed us to run down for a few moments before breakfast. Our "few moments before breakfast" became hours of exploration. There were so many new things to discover!

Translucent jelly fish lying in little masses in the sun, drift wood, sea shells and chubby little sand crabs burrowing into wet sand as each glistening wave slid from shore and yes...the waves, white capped and enchanting to a poetic child, crashing about my feet, then up to my knees until finally, fully clothed, I was, (despite my mother's forebodings), immersed in the sea. But she was also in her element, soul sisters that we were, as well as mother and daughter, for as long as I can remember.

Were my siblings even there that day...I know they were. But I was in a world apart, lost in a dream of wonder. I do recall my youngest brother, Jonathan, his little legs barely keeping up with mine as we ran to the water's edge... but I had set out on my own to discover what was to become a lifelong love of mine...the sea.

Each day was the same, the joy constant. My skin turned brown and my body got plump from experiencing new delights...lobster, crab legs and scallops.

There was an amusement park nearby which we often visited in the evenings. My sister and I always road the Ferris wheel facing out over the ocean. As we floated skyward, we caught glimpses of the moon painting silver paths through the water...and I was at peace.

I recall long afternoons in the waves with my little brothers. My oldest brother being, as he has remained throughout my life, just a little bit out of reach and my mother and sister lying in the sun coaxing their fair skin to darken.

One day in the distance, I saw my father walking toward us. Suddenly I was aware that all the ladies lying in the sun around us were watching him. Purposely, I saw him through a stranger's eyes and knew that hearts quickened at the sight of this man, lean and tan in this Navy dress whites. I ran to meet him, taking his hand, always secure in its grip and so proud on that particular day, heads turning as we passed, that he was my father and so very handsome.

Brevity will not allow me to describe every detail of that wonderful summer. A trip to Colonial Williamsburg where I first smelled lavender, my brother's appendectomy when officers' wives brought ice packs and medical advice as he lay twisting in pain until Dad sped him to the Naval hospital in Portsmouth where emergency surgery was performed.

A storm one day over the ocean when lights went out and ice cream melted in freezers, followed by a soul penetrating calm.

The Ocean...the ever-beating heat... contracting and relaxing, always in motion, as the human heart is constantly in motion until the day of death...and now they tell us that the sea, too, is dying.

It was the last vacation we ever took together as a family, divorce separated us several years later. My father is gone now, stricken with cancer in the spring of 1987. Still fairly young...and still handsome.

One August I took my brother's young daughters to the sea. They had never been before, so I tried to see it as they were seeing it...through their innocent eyes. They were enchanted. I was reminded of another summer many years earlier and seeing the ocean for the first time with their father...his little legs scarcely keeping up with mine as we ran to the water's edge...and I wanted to share it with you.

Me & my brothers, Walter & Joe

IF

If I were a laughing child today
I'd run down to the sea and play.
The gulls would call me from my bed,
I'd shake a golden, tousled head
And readily obey.

A grey and misty morn would be
The very thing for little me
My chubby legs would run and I
Would leap for joy beneath the sky.

If I were but a child again,
The years erasing present pain
I'd commune with sand and seas
Shimmering in a gentle rain,
Whispering on a morning breeze.

The smell of warm, salt air would rise
Enveloping the earth and skies
And all the very soul of me
Would FEEL this...day.

If only we could wander backward
Through the pain,
To a young girl dancing
In the rain.

"I've seen fire and I've seen rain
I've seen sunny days
That I thought would never end
I've seen lonely times
When I could not find a friend...
But I always thought
That I'd see you again."

James Taylor

Layla

LAYLA

Beauty is a rarity in fourteen-year-old girls. It's such an awkward age. But Layla was gorgeous. Her grandfather was African American and her mother a beautiful, olive skinned Mulatto woman.

Layla looked like her mother...tall and thin with long brown hair, arched eyebrows, great lips and that awesome complexion. And she had a sharp tongue, too. A real contender in an argument...and a deep, rich laugh. She could melt you with kindness or sting like a scorpion. I don't know why I wasn't jealous of her.

She lived way out in the country with her mother (a former runway model), several siblings and a wickedly handsome, but shiftless father. I remember he played in a rock and roll band.

We drew close to each other that fourteenth year of our lives...and watched our families crumble around our ears.

One sultry July day my mother sat me and my sister down and told us that she and Dad were getting a divorce. She seemed sad and defeated. My sister cried. She said she didn't want our mother to grow old alone.

This was the year of my first (and last) high school Prom. I had been voted in for the court. This was the last thing I wanted to do, since "The Doors" were playing in Pittsburgh that night and my sister and I were planning to go.

But I put on my "big girl panties," a little lipstick, fluffed my hair and asked a boy to be my escort. When he arrived that evening to take me to the dance, I passed my parents on the way downstairs. He had her by the arm and was saying something angry and menacing. She looked frightened. I felt helpless. This was my first prom. I was in a satin gown and platform shoes, instead of my usual jeans and t-shirt. They didn't even see me.

The bright lights of the gymnasium were a blur as I went through the motions of the coronation. The boy whose arm I clung to was practically a stranger. I knew I wasn't like the other girls. I looked out into the bleachers and saw parents...in pairs...cameras in hand, snapping pictures of their beautiful daughters.

I left my date that night, without a word, all alone in the school gym. I walked home, the hem of my gown dragging through the mud and went straight to bed. This was the beginning of a long bout with depression...a recurring theme throughout my life.

The hardest thing about my parents' divorce was the loss of my mother. She had always been a "stay at home" mom but was now thrown into the workplace. I know this was a necessary buffer against poverty...but I missed her. I will give my dad this...he never missed a child-support payment.

Layla didn't fare so well in the dissolution of her family, as she and her siblings were thrown into one bad situation after another. Once her mom ran off with a married man, taking her children with her. For months they traveled around the country staying in one cheap hotel after another, until "Clyde" ran out of money and went begging back to his merciful wife.

Layla and I bonded in the chaos. We spent long afternoons running through fields or sitting on the creek bank smoking pot or planning our "big get away". We couldn't decide whether that would happen by running away or committing suicide. Of course, we had no real intention of doing either...but obviously, escape from our circumstances seemed desirable. In the end, it was she who got away...for one humid summer afternoon an old van drove up to our house. Layla, her mother, brothers and sisters and a young hippie couple who befriended them, had come to say goodbye. They were moving to a commune in Northern California.

Watching that van pull away and knowing that I may never see her again was heart wrenching. And for sure, it was the end of an innocent age for us both.

One night several years later, soon after I had married, I heard a knock at my door and there in the darkness stood my old friend...still so beautiful...and we had what turned out to be our last visit together. Layla died of cancer when she was 28 years old...leaving two precious children behind. It is my pleasure to be connected to her beautiful daughter on Facebook. Her youngest granddaughter looks just like her. The cycle of life continues... Layla would be so proud.

One day as I sat flipping through the pages of Time magazine, I was stunned by the photograph of a beautiful young woman. She had long, dark hair, flawless skin and arched brows. And she was dead. Killed in crossfire in some war-torn country, and I thought "Layla."

On the domed glass lid of her coffin someone had scrawled, "I'll never forget you, I love you."

When I think of her now, we are always girls again, wading through frigid streams, roaming green Pennsylvania hills and playing like tomorrow would never come. But come it did...

I'll never forget you.

I love you.

NANCY INGRID HURD

DOCTOR MARISKA

Summer memories sweep over me tonight. The year was 1969 and my sister, cousin Kathy, two younger brothers and I were sweltering and bored in our house beside West Greene High School. Suddenly, unexpectedly, we saw through the screen door my Father's eccentric friend, Dr. Mariska, pulling up in his old Chevy station wagon. He had come to rescue his ol' pal's children from summer doldrums by taking us berry picking up the holler...and we were bored enough to go. It was a brilliant strategy really...he kept all the berries.

At some point I walked down to the car for water and there was my brother, ten years old at the time, sitting on the tailgate with a Rolling Rock in his hand.

"I am teaching Walter an important lesson", Dr Mariska explained, "when he is a big boy and goes off to college, bad boys will try to entice him to drink alcohol the wrong way. I am showing him that there is a right, responsible way."

"Are you learning your lesson, Walt?" I asked...he grinned and looked like the cat who had just swallowed the canary.

The same Dr. Mariska threw a dead groundhog in our yard that summer, barely slowing down as he tossed the carcass from his car window. My Mother, incensed, called him that evening demanding an explanation. "I thought you could have it for your dinner," he said, sounding genuinely offended..." they really are quite tender when young."

NANCY INGRID HURD

DEPARTURE

Leading up to my Dad's leaving, we were all walking on eggshells, as tension between my parents built. I pictured a balloon expanded beyond capacity and thought..." somebody pop this thing! Somebody just POP it!"

He started spending more and more nights sleeping on a cot in his office. Then one evening he came home and stood briefly by the front door glaring at my mother, who continued washing dishes without looking up. After a few minutes, he reached into his inner coat pocket and drew out five envelopes with a name written on each of them, Joe, Greta, Nancy, Walter and Jonathan. Then with great disdain he said, "give these to the kids on Christmas morning, since I am no longer a member of this family."

I was standing by the bar, witnessing all of this. I wanted to hug him, shake him and scream, "Act right and you can stay! Just act right!"

My heart was breaking for him, but I was angry, too. I knew that he had caused this breach and I knew how he had done it and that he could fix it. I also knew that he wouldn't or couldn't SEE what he had done. Pride broke his home. After that we didn't see Dad for what seemed like a very long time.

I remember walking with my sister through College Park one day and she pointed to a house and said, "Dad lives up there." I didn't feel sad, just perplexed that he had just disappeared and was living like a stranger. I slowed my step as we passed, trying to picture what he might be doing in there. I sensed that he was very depressed, and I was right.

One day after the chaos in our home began to die down and Mom was working, Dad showed up at our door with a six-pack of "Klondike" bars from Isaly's restaurant and dairy bar. He seemed different, lighter...friendlier, kinder. I was happy to see him...and glad to get the ice cream. After that he came weekly with his signature Klondike bars.

Then one day he asked me if I would be interested in cleaning his house a couple of times a month and he would pay me. So...that was the beginning of a new relationship with Dad. We kept the "cleaning" arrangement up for a while, then more and more my younger brothers and I began visiting because we enjoyed hanging out with him. Enjoyed the newfound freedom to roam all over Waynesburg untethered...the fish stick and canned pea dinners by candlelight, the "Pepperidge Farm" cakes...our unexpected friendship with our Father.

I have always been an introvert, but somehow collected an entourage of friends both old and new, whose companionship got me through the crazy years.

Ruby...Dear Ruby! With the mane of long, red hair and a heart wide enough to understand everything.

Marlys, who looked up at me from her painting in advanced art class one day and said matter-of-factly, "Let's become fast friends." And we did.

Then there were Tena, Lisa, Patty and Peggy. Laughter made our days brighter. The ascent from darkness had begun.

THE HOUDINI CHAIR

What do four kids do, (brother Joe had joined the Navy) on long summer days when nearly all parental guidance and restrictions have been lifted? ...Anything they want to.

One August afternoon the phone rang and it was Mr. Henner, the local Boy Scout leader calling to remind my brothers that there would be a meeting that evening.

I think most of our neighbors weren't yet aware that conditions had deteriorated in the Hurd household. The boys had been missing most of their meetings and dear Mr. Henner kept calling with reminders and encouragement. I heard Walter in the kitchen expressing doubt that he and Jon would be able to attend that night's meeting. Then he walked into the TV room where Greta, Jon and I were watching "Dark Shadows", our favorite creepy day time drama. Walter looked sheepish and said that he wished Mr. Henner would stop calling.

"But Walt," I mused, "you've learned such useful things in Boy Scouts." "Like what?" he asked drolly, "Like knot tying." I said. "Yeah, I can tie a pretty good knot," Walter conceded. "I can tie knots that no one could ever escape from."

Greta jumped up and grabbed a kitchen chair, placing it in the middle of the room. "I'll bet I can," she said, "tie me up and I'll prove it to you."

So, Walter and Jon put their heads together, deciding on the best knot for the job, as Greta sat with hands behind her back. Within minutes she was free. "Let's see if I can escape," I said, as I took my place on the "Houdini" chair. Again, Walter and Jon gave it their best shot, but within minutes I was free. "Now let us tie you up," Greta said...so Walt sat down while Greta and I went to work on him.

The knots were very secure. Walter worked and worked and struggled...but our knots held fast...so we tied his feet together too, then removing the bandana from his jeans pocket, proceeded to gag him. He fought like a madman...getting angrier by the minute, but we had outdone ourselves. At this point one of us got the brilliant idea to carry Walter and the Houdini chair out by the side of the road and leave him there.

It was glorious watching him from the window. Walt would struggle like mad until a car rounded the curve...then he would sit with head held high, mustering every ounce of dignity he possessed, until the car passed, then he would start the struggle again. Finally, after quite a while, he was free and mad as hell.

Greta and I ran through the house locking all the doors and windows until Walt had a chance to cool off. Eventually, with his solemn promise not to take vengeance on us if we let him in, the door was unlocked, and an angry Walter stomped up the stairs to his room. This was one of many crazy antics at the Hurd House that summer, but the only one that I am going to disclose.

"I see my light
Come shining
From the West
Unto the East
Any day now,
Any day now,
I shall be released."

Bob Dylan

REDEMPTION

**My friend Linda with
husband, Bob 1974**

Me in 1973

REDEMPTION

I've always been in a kind of awe...and fear...of my body. Ever since that night in 1960 when my parents went out for the evening, leaving us in the care of Nancy Bollock, a negligent babysitter.

I loved testing my limits when not being watched, so Greta and I sneaked into the bathroom and I climbed up drawers to reach the top of a dresser where medicine was kept well out of reach of "good" children and grabbed a large bottle of Bayer aspirin. I poured many pills into a glass of water and started drinking. It tasted something like Alka Seltzer, which I like, so I downed the entire glass of white, cloudy, aspirin infused water...then crept back to bed.

Thankfully, my mother had a headache when she and Dad got home that night and went immediately into the bathroom to find that the once full aspirin bottle was nearly empty. I remember Mom coming into our room and asking, "who took the aspirin?" Greta could truthfully say that she had not, but always keen to avoid trouble, I lied.

"Whoever took that aspirin," my mother said sternly, "will be dead in the morning." I am not exaggerating when I say that I literally "saw" black. I knew what dead meant; I had seen our old cat Tinkerbell lying dead by the curb at the end of our street a couple of years earlier.

"Oh Mommy," I was so frightened I could barely speak..." I did it."

She pulled me out of bed and called Dr. Cuba, who instructed her to make me drink glass after glass of water, then stick her fingers down my throat until I vomited. He said to continue this until there was no more "white" in the toilet water. So, she and Dad put me through this torture, water... gag... vomit... repeat... until every trace of aspirin was gone, and we were all exhausted.

Then she placed me between them in their bed and held me tight as I went into a deep sleep. I am sure she kept vigil over me all through the night.

I still remember how happy I was when I awoke in the morning. I remember what I ate for breakfast...I remember what I wore. The sun seemed brighter. I had been spared...but ever after, I was somehow wary of my body.

My physical health was never terribly good but not terribly bad either. I just lived in a kind of limited physiological twilight, stuck in this clay vessel while longing for "the glorious freedom of the sons of God." I'm weird. I know.

I will never forget the summer of my 16th year. My friend Linda, who was 4 years older than I, came home to PA for an extended visit after moving to Palo Alto, California, during the thick of the hippie movement, bringing with her a new way to experience life and food.

I knew through TV that there were "health nuts" in the world who subsisted on tofu and watercress sandwiches; but when Linda came home with books written by later 19th century health guru, Arnold Ehrett, and multigrain muffins from the original "Barbara's Bakery" in Palo Alto where her fiancé worked, I was converted.

Under Linda's tutelage with ease and delight, Greta and I gave up all the staple foods of our childhood. Out with the meat, glutenous casseroles, soda pop, milk and bologna sandwiches...in with brewer's yeast, soybeans (considered a health food in the early 70's), home baked whole wheat bread and incredible fresh salads with every raw veggie we could find at our local A&P.

There was no such thing as "organically grown" in Waynesburg in 1971, but we made do with what was available, and felt our bodies purge years of toxic build up, as new lightness and clarity of mind, body and spirit emerged.

It felt good. It was an awakening. I was happy. It wasn't just the new way of eating that brought about this change...it was everything about Linda.

Greta and I had sunk into a sort of oblivion after our parents' divorce; we all had. Joe escaped to the Navy, Greta and I escaped to bad habits, while our poor little brothers were left to kind of fend for themselves.

I wish with all my heart that I had possessed the maturity to understand what Jon and Walter were going through during those turbulent years, but I was a kid too, acting out in destructive ways, and oblivious to anyone's trouble but my own. I regret this very much.

But Linda came and rescued us. I dare say she may have saved my life that summer. She definitely saved my butt.

I had already given up drugs and alcohol by this time...I did that on my own, without the help of any adult in my life...but was still in a very dark place.

Immediately upon her arrival, Linda, who practically lived with us that summer, put a stop to the madness. She was a sister, mother, mentor and friend. No more pot, cigarettes, junk food, "killing these miraculous bodies is just not cool" she said. And I really listened.

Greta learned to sew that year, bake wonderful breads and created beautiful hippie dresses for us from fabrics purchased in the basement of Murphy's "five and dime". Off went make-up, bras and shoes. On went those gorgeous dresses. With renewed health and vitality my hair grew clear to my waist.

We ran through fields, baked nutritious bread and filled the summer of my 16th year with the music of James Taylor, Joni Mitchell, Bob Dylan, Elton John, George Harrison, B.B. King, Carole King, Hot Tuna and Traffic. Oh...and laugher...lots and lots of laughter.

As long as I live, and I had the privilege of telling her this in recent years, I will be grateful to my friend Linda Patton Johnson, who came all the way across the continental USA and with humor and kindness whipped two wayward girls into shape. Thanks, my friend.

Do you know I love ya? Well, I do.

MUSIC IN THE PARK

Waynesburg University can boast of an impressive park system...well maintained and beautiful, with an abundance of massive, luxuriant old growth trees. There is in the center of the park, an antiquated and ornate fountain, where we used to gather to play guitars or toss frisbees in the early seventies and later, with my sister and our little girls; Alexus, Rebecca and Mary in tow, we would watch with delight as they stripped to their undies and played with wild abandon in the cascading water.

I can close my eyes and "look" down the sprawling green to "Lake Juanita", a mere pond really, surrounded by verdant rushes and covered in lily pads. At one time, it was inhabited by some discarded goldfish, which untethered by the confines of a little bowl, grew to the size of catfish.

To my right, overseeing the park like sentinels are the two oldest buildings on campus, Hannah and Miller Halls. My father's office was in Miller Hall...the more ornate of the two and I have fond memories of exploring her hallways...admiring her massive wooden staircase and sneaking up those stairs to the attic, where many wonderful historical artifacts can probably be found to this day.

When the young men of Waynesburg began drifting back into town after their time in Viet Nam, although only in my mid-teens at the time, I could sense the unease they brought home with them. Clearly, they had been traumatized. Most returned quietly back on the scene sporting awkward military crew cuts...which gradually grew and grew and grew... at least this was the case with the hippie guys my sister and I befriended.

None spoke openly of their time in "Nam" and no one asked questions...but they were all hurting. One young man was memorable. He had a bush of long brown hair, wore a ring in one ear as was common in those days, and had a small

American flag wrapped around the ankle of his faded and patched bell-bottom jeans.

He was quiet and mysterious...barely spoke...but when he did, looked right through you with those piercing dark eyes and said something profound. Mostly he stayed to himself and watched the rest of us...making calculations, it seemed, and we admired him from a distance, for all his mysterious depths and solitude...because he was fascinating.

Somewhere in his travels he had obtained a flute. He had never played a flute before and had no formal training. But he spent hours...sometimes long into the night...some said all night, pouring the saddest and most enchanting music through the park. A colleague of my Dad's, John Holleran, said he opened his windows at night and listened to the haunting music.

I could picture him there, alone in the darkness, healing his inner wounds in this way. Once I heard him and was reminded of a "Popeye" cartoon I had seen, where the old Seahag stood on a precipice and played just like this on her magic flute, silhouetted against an enormous moon.

And then...one night the music stopped as mysteriously as it had started, never to be heard again. Who WAS this young man? Where did life take him?

He and my sister fell in love and got married. After years of struggling with his demons, he stabilized, becoming a man of faith and respectability. He fathered four beautiful, caring daughters, had a meaningful career in the medical field and now; nearly fifty years later, remains married to my sister, who still adores him.

"You'll walk unscathed
Through musket fire
No ploughman's blade
Will cut thee down...
No cutlass wound
Will mark thy face,
And you will be my 'ain true love...
And you will be my 'ain true love...

Gordon Sumner, Sting

NANCY INGRID HURD

marriage & children...etc.

With my babies, Rebecca & Neil

"...I had a king in
A salt rusted carriage,
Carried me off to his country
For marriage too soon...
Beware of the power of moon!...

...I can't go back there anymore,
You know my keys won't fit the door
And all my thoughts don't fit the man...
They never can...
They never can"

J. Mitchell

With Dad on my Wedding Day, 1974

MARRIAGE

By all accounts it was a beautiful wedding. October 13th, 1974 was a glorious Autumn day, right in the thick of an unusually warm "Indian Summer". My mother's backyard was the perfect venue for my hippie wedding and a winding cement walkway ending beneath a huge elm tree made an ideal outdoor aisle.

My dear friend, Marlys, an art major at Penn State University, had come the day before and spent an afternoon gathering wild autumn flowers on the hill behind my mother's house, creating beautiful fall motif bouquets and filling two wooden barrels with ivy, wild weeds, vine, leaf and filigree. The effect was truly lovely, for a "poor man's" wedding.

Mrs. Warrick, our neighbor and local seamstress...the same lady who had made my prom dress several years earlier, created a gorgeous cotton gown of autumn colors...gold, brown, russet and forest green...I adorned my waist length long hair with a satin ribbon and cheap wide brimmed straw hat from our local Murphy's "five and dime", threw on some leather sandals and Voilà! Here comes the bride.

We dragged our old wooden stereo into the yard and played the most beautiful symphony I could find in my mother's modest vinyl collection. Dad was distinguished as always as he escorted me down the ivy strewn walkway, and all of our oldest friends and a few relatives filled our yard, dressed in their Sunday best, to share in the day's festivities.

And festive it was! We roasted a pig, emptied a keg, and danced until late in the evening.

But I knew as I strolled down that winding walkway on my father's arm, the man who waited for me beneath the sprawling elm tree was not the one I had dreamed of. He had pursued me with such a vengeance...stalking by today's terms...and sadly, I was rebounding from the one I had loved and lost.

I was so immature, barely nineteen, and didn't understand what I was entering into...the finality of it...nor did I understand the brutal effects of alcoholism, a disease he was in the throes of...so I married him, naively thinking it would break the heart of my beloved, who had chosen another girl over me. (Someone I have come to like and respect very much...time heals everything.) But in the end, the only heart that I had broken was my own.

To Mark

The years pass by so quickly,
Losing things we can't replace.
I can see it in the mirror
And the lines upon your face
And you'd think that we'd grow wiser,
Seems we'd come to understand
What it takes to love each other
Heart to heart...and hand in hand.
I lift my face to your face
Drawing closer for a kiss...
As usual, I feel the pull...
My stubborn heart resists.
I've tried to take it captive,
Make it do the things it ought
But the rebel always runs
Determined never to be caught.
It can't surrender in a swamp
While crying for the sea,
I think it's needing more from love
Than you can give to me.

1987

Mysteries unravel on the page before me
As they christen my existence
With their triumph and sorrow.
I stand, almost unable to move
As I stare at my page
In this book of humanity.
Must one care about a happy ending
When their tears are the ink
And their blood illustrates the page?
Urban legends, mythical characters,
Watercolors, still-life, mystery, poetry and prose.
How this dance of life will spill out
On your page-
No one ever really knows.

Rebecca (Rush) Klein 2000

My beautiful Rebecca today with son, Owen and husband, Daniel

Rebecca, Wedding Day

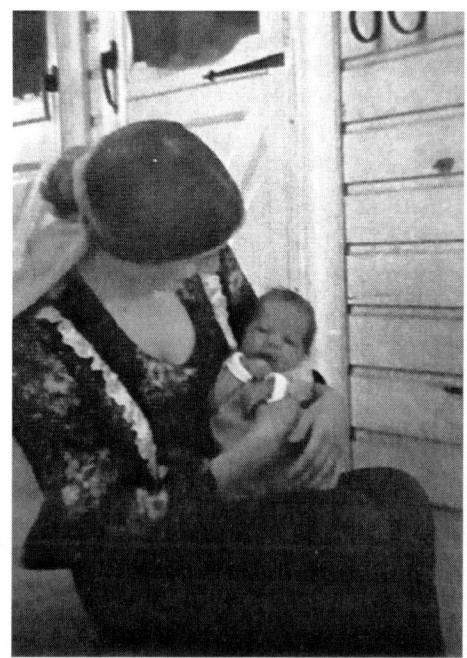

Rebecca & Owen

REBECCA

As I mentioned before, in the Autumn of 1974, after a whirlwind romance, I married a troubled and troublesome man. I still bear scars from that ungodly alliance with a raging alcoholic. He chased me down and I wasn't strong enough to resist his advances. (Where was my father?) We were married for fourteen chaotic years. But something wonderful came of that union...my beloved children, Rebecca and Neil.

I was barely twenty when my first born came. I knew that mothers love their children. But I had always held my heart close and never expected to give it all away...she was...she is...the light of my world.

The pregnancy was hard...I developed "toxemia" (I believe it's called "preeclampsia" now.) My body was swollen, and my kidneys compromised, so the doctor ordered complete bedrest for the last month of pregnancy. I just knew my husband would understand and take care of me, so I went home that afternoon and settled into my bed with a mound of pillows and stacks of books and magazines. The window was open, and a pleasant July breeze floated in, causing the lace curtains to billow. It was pleasant and I was happy.

Later that evening Mark came home angry, drunk and belligerent. He had been in a fight uptown and there was blood on his shirt. He raged through our apartment screaming and throwing things...all my pretty knick-knacks shattered across the kitchen floor. When he finally stormed out, I called my sister who came for me and drove me to our mother's house. There I was cared for very well for the next few days.

Then one evening he called...calm, sober, remorseful...and asked me to come home. He said the apartment was clean and he was grilling chicken outside. He begged me to return. I was nine months pregnant, unwell and didn't know what else to do. So, I went home...he was clean shaven, well dressed and kind.

The house was orderly, supper was good. I ate and went to sleep.

In the morning, July 20th, 1975, the phone rang, and it was Dr. Cruz, who sounded concerned. She told me to shower, pack a bag and meet her at the hospital. I braided by long hair so it wouldn't tangle during labor and delivery, as my sister had suggested. During my shower I ran my hand over my big tummy and thought "from this day forward I will be a mother and totally responsible for the life of another person." A thought that both excited and terrified me.

When we reached the hospital, sensing my father's stability, Dr Cruz directed her words to him and away from my husband. She said that I was in a delicate state and was anxious for the pregnancy to be over. She would break my water and if that didn't bring labor on, she was going to induce with an IV. We went into a treatment room where she inserted a long plastic hook and ruptured the placenta. I immediately felt the trickle of warm water and mild cramping. By the time she got me back to my room we could clock the minutes between pains and by early evening I was in full blown labor.

Everyone in my family came to witness the big event. My Dad and his 2nd wife, my mother, sister and sister-in-law. Even my little brothers were there...heavy stuff for teenage boys...so when my friend's mother, who was also head of maternity came and shooed everyone but my mom, sister and husband away, I was relieved.

The pain kept increasing in intensity until after 10:00, when something remarkable and unexpected happened. I began pushing, involuntarily, with all my might. No one had told me about "pushing" and I was overwhelmed! Soon, a nurse counted 10cm and began rushing me down the hall toward the open doors of the delivery room. I passed frantic looking family members on the way. Mom looked calm and comforting, but Dad was ashen colored and biting his lip. I wanted so much to tell him I was OK...but screamed and "pushed" instead. Poor man!

In the delivery room they did their archaic worst...strapping my hands and feet down to the table. From there, through a mirror on the ceiling, I watched with wonder...as if it were happening to someone else... the birth of my first-born child.

Afterward they gave me something to knock me out and I faded into a white, painless wonderful oblivion. The next thing I remember, my mother was standing over me saying, "Nancy, you have a little girl." "A girl..." I repeated. I was exhausted and happier than I've ever been.

Mark was standing outside the nursery window craning his neck this way and that, trying to see his new baby girl from every angle. He ran into my room, kissed me and said very sincerely, "thank you honey, for having my baby."

Soon Mrs. Goodwin, a nurse and our neighbor, came sailing in smiling from ear to ear, with a little pink bundle in her arms. It was plain to see she was delighted to introduce us. "Here she is honey," she said, "she is just perfect! See...she has all her little fingers and her little toes..."and for the first time, I laid eyes on my beautiful girl. Immediately I pulled the blanket away and admired her perfect face and plump little body. I held her for the longest time...telling her over and over again how happy I was to meet her and singing all the lullabies I knew from my childhood. I tried to nurse her, but she only wanted to lay close and listen to my voice...and struggled to open her eyes. She was anxious to see me, too. Finally, Mrs. Goodwin reappeared and whisked her off to the nursery, leaving me alone with my thoughts.

I went to sleep so grateful that she had finally come and was healthy and safe. But I also had a foreboding that with Mark's alcoholism, hard times were ahead. I wanted to place her in a glass bubble where nothing and no one could ever harm her...and I knew that as long as I lived, I would strive to protect, nurture and love my beautiful daughter. And to the best of my ability, I did.

She is a woman now with a child of her own. She is a wonderful wife, exceptional mother and caring daughter. She has traveled and had an interesting career in the medical field. She is a considerate, capable, good person.

The day of her birth, July 20th, 1975 is forever fixed in my mind...as stars are fixed in the night sky. When I no longer remember my middle name, I will remember that beautiful night when Mrs. Goodwin came running in, all smiles, and lay my first-born child in my arms. The night I truly understood the meaning of love.

Rebecca, I am so sorry for all the chaos. Please know this...that little voice inside your head...your father's voice that keeps saying you aren't good enough, is a colossal lie. You are good enough...and one of the finest people I have ever known. So, give yourself permission to live your life with abundance and joy. You have the right to be happy. And it's what you deserve.

I am sorry for making some bad decisions that impacted our family negatively; for all the ways I might have hurt you. I didn't mean to. Most of all I am sorry for the apology your father was never able to give.

But I am so blessed to be your mother, and so grateful...I love you forever.
-Mom

To Rebecca Dawn...Dancing (5 years old)

She danced across a sun swept floor
With gold dust in her hair
Her eyes enraptured...radiant...
Her partner...Fred Astaire
Then curtsied low to the TV
And no one believes that
I know I saw him wink at her...
And lightly tip his hat.

1980

**Father's mother, Nola Barbe Hurd
(Rebecca's great grandmother)**

WAITING

By Rebecca Rush Klein
2000

Some say that the window to the soul is the eyes. I, however, have always believed it to be in the hands.

I remember as a young girl I used to sit on my mother's lap and gaze intently at her hands. I can still see them so clearly, long slender fingers, short clean nails and a thin white gold band on her left ring finger, passed down from her grandmother and my great, on her father's side.

Neither one of us had ever seen more than a photograph of her...an aged black and white photo of a tall, thin, well dressed young woman with milky white skin and black hair, on some steps of a large brick house. I never asked where the picture was taken, nor whom she was posing for. The picture remains a mystery to me to this day, as I suppose will she. I do remember thinking she appeared to be waiting for something or better yet, someone. Her white hands folded in front of her, her fingers loosely clutching the handle of a small purse. Her face was calm and smiling...her eyes confident, as if she was sure they would come.

My mother used to often remind me that the ring had belonged to my great grandmother. Proudly pulling out the picture and allowing me to look...perhaps because my mother was such a historian...or because it was more pleasant to discuss her late grandmother than it was to discuss her marriage to my father, that the ring had come to represent.

I remember holding up my own hands, comparing their soft youthful skin to the hard-working hands of my mother...with the self-assurance of a child that they would never age as hers had, or bear the brunt of time.

At twenty-five I sit and look at my hands, with the confidence of a woman that one day they will nurture children, hold the hand of a partner and work hard for a family, as did my mother. And as I stand waiting, much like the woman in the picture, my wish is never to neglect the present...and never forget the past.

The Little Dolls

The Grown-Up Dolls

Sara, Alexus, Rebecca, Mary

THE DOLLS

Try to go back for just a little while...through the looking glass...through the veil...like Alice, or the Lady of Shallot. It's a dangerous place if you linger there...the glass will crack, and the spell will come upon you.

Tonight, I remember four little girls. They are sitting on the bottom step in the kitchen of my "Bowlby Street" house, with their grandfather, who is holding the youngest, Baby Sara. The other girls hold new dolls in their arms, beautifully handmade by my sister. Each doll has yarn hair, the color of its possessor. Yellow for Rebecca, red for Mary and black for Alexus. All are smiling and wearing new clothes, for it is a party day. I have had a "Holly Hobbie" cake baked for the special occasion.

Whatever happened to those unique and very beautiful dolls?

All are married now and have children of their own.

NANCY INGRID HURD

He fell down
Through the heavens...
He fell into the cracks
And crevices in sidewalks
Where we break our mother's backs.
Then lifted like a fever
Breaking sweat in quiet dawn
And purged himself of everything
That never did belong

-N.H.

Robert Joseph Hurd, doing what he loved.

FREE-FALLING

Dad loved jumping out of airplanes and target shooting after dark (to hone night vision) and sleeping on hard porch benches when mercury was in the teens (to test his endurance). He was a man who enjoyed pushing the limits.

So, none of us were surprised when he, a man in his forties, retired as a commander in the Naval Reserves and joined the Green Beret's. To be specific, 2nd Battalion, 19th Special Forces, and he prided himself on being "airborne".

One evening my brother Jon and I were watching TV in Dad's living room when he descended the stairs in full uniform, sporting his jaunty green beret. Addressing my brother, he asked, "Jonathan, looking at a man, how would you know if he was "airborne?".

Quickly scanning his uniform for clues, Jon answered..." uh...broken legs?" ...yeah, that was funny. But what happened on the night of November 19th, 1976, was not.

In the early morning hours of November 20th, my sister called and spoke the words that I had always dreaded..." Dad has been in an accident." She said. Fearing the worst, I asked, "Is he dead?" and held my breath.

"No," she replied, "but badly injured." "What happened?" I asked, "Will he be alright?" she continued..." Last night he was sky diving...on maneuvers with his unit near Morgantown, WV and his parachute didn't open."

Trying to wrap my mind around what she had just said, I envisioned him falling into a canopy of treetops, or a pond or marsh land.

But no, he hit the solid ground in November. And lived.

"He crushed his 5th thoracic vertebrae" she said, "and he is badly shaken up. But they think he will be okay." It was unbelievable...

Hurriedly, I gathered up my baby girl and headed for West Virginia University Hospital, (now Ruby Memorial), in Morgantown, where he had been rushed the night before. He had spent the night in intensive care, but when I arrived, had already been transferred to a floor.

It was heart wrenching to see him so injured. Every breath was excruciating. One vertebra crushed and his body full of contusions inside and out, but he was alive. Doctors and nurses where coming in and out of his room...some who were not even on his case...to lay eyes on their "miracle" patient.

A nurse stuck her head in the door and said, "Mr. Hurd, there is another international call for you. Do you feel like taking it?" No, he did not, but couldn't resist. It was one of his former students calling from Japan, where he had seen the report of Dad's incredible experience on the news.

Between naps and various interruptions, I was able to piece together what had occurred on that fateful night.

Night jumping was a fairly routine maneuver. On this particular evening, the C-1, 30 Hercules plane which was carrying them, dropped her passengers one by one as usual. But when it came time for Dad's free fall to end with the usual whoosh and upward jolt of the opening parachute, he realized in horror that this did not happen. Instead, his chute was an unopened streamer of tangled rope and fabric, whipping about in the night sky.

Next move was to pull the rip cord on his reserve chute located in front of him in what is called a "belly pack". The reserve chute does not open with as much force as the main chute (at least not in 1976), so he pushed it out and away from him, with all his might. Unbelievably, it didn't open either, but got tangled up in the flagging main chute instead.

Unafraid, he quickly assumed the position he was taught to take in such an emergency. Body as upright as possible and knees slightly bent. Fleetingly, he thought of his family and how hard this was going to be on all of us. Then he hit the ground.

A searing pain tore through his spine...as he lay on the still, cold ground on someone's farm in West Virginia, waiting for death to come. Unbelievably...he never went unconscious. Assessing the damage, he found he could move his hands and feet ever so slightly. This was a good sign.

Soon, he could hear a siren in the distance. He was relieved, but still felt certain that he was about to die. The paramedics carefully loaded him into the ambulance. On the way to the hospital, still fully conscious, he began to believe that perhaps he was going to live after all...and felt over whelmingly grateful.

And how grateful *we* were not to have lost our Dad that night. He wore a body cast for a couple of months, and all his upper dental work dislodged and had to be redone and he was an inch and a half shorter for the remaining 13 years of his life.

But the biggest changes occurred within the man himself. In his heart. He was a bit more fragile...a bit more thoughtful...more in tune to his feelings and those of his family...a kinder, gentler man.

He had seen that we are, as he told me later, "dangling from a thin thread" and can be taken very suddenly...so he learned to value the important things. That was the unexpected gift that he and we were given through this harrowing experience.

One day, the "National Enquirer" called, seeking Dad's permission to print his story. He didn't care for their particular brand of journalism and declined.

"We are going to print it with or without your permission" he was told candidly. "With permission you get $300 dollars. Without permission you get nothing." So...permission was granted and three hundred donated to Waynesburg College. His story also appeared in the Canadian edition of "Reader's Digest".

Our family appreciated dearly, this 2nd chance with our father.

I believe the remaining years of his life were relatively calm and happy. But his days of taking unnecessary risks were over. Except for the occasional camp out on a hard porch bench in subfreezing weather.

Some things just never change.

"Riders on the storm,
Riders on the storm,
Into this house we're born
Into this world we're thrown." [7]

J. Morrison

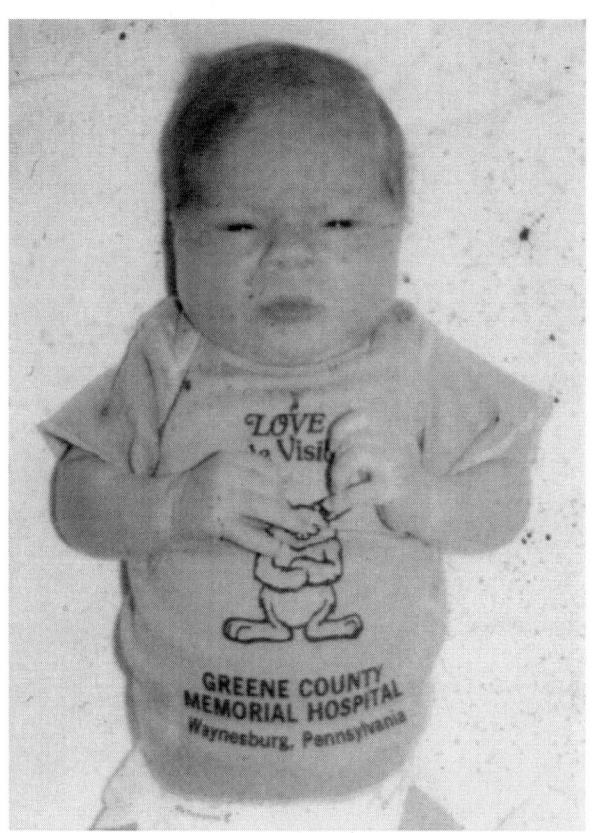

Neil, on the day he was born

**My son, Neil Andrew Rush, with
daughter, Cora**

NEIL – RIDER ON THE STORM

After the birth of my daughter, I decided emphatically, "Never again!" She, of course, was wonderful. But Mark's drinking was out of control and let's face it... childbirth hurts. So, for 5 years I was settled in my mind to be the mother of an "only child".

Then things changed. I began to daydream about soft, chubby bodies and velvety little heads. I could almost smell a baby. And Rebecca began praying daily for a "little brother or sister", even asking once if we could buy one off the black market. Also, Mark was attending AA meetings, which gave me hope.

I remember the day I returned home from the doctor with my news...a bun was definitely in the oven! Mark was happy, Rebecca overjoyed.

Pregnancy was pretty awful. Mark quit going to AA and stayed drunk most of the time. Night after night I lie in bed until all hours, my baby churning inside of me, while he partied. I rubbed by hands over by growing tummy, telling this little one how sorry I was and that I loved him... (or her) ...back then you never knew what you were getting. But I was sure it was a boy and I knew he must be in turmoil, since I was. I just didn't have the skills to stop the madness...but somehow, we got through it.

On the eve of October 10th, 1981 my mother stopped in for a visit. She took one look at me and said, "Nan, it's time, you're about to have the baby. There's something different about you tonight." Within minutes, I passed the cervical plug and labor began. Although mild, Mom decided to spend the night. I had made Mark move out several weeks earlier and I was grateful for her company. She was always there when I needed her. I had light cramping through the night and was able to sleep comfortably.

October 11, 1981 at 7:00 AM I awoke to sharp pains that could be clocked at regular intervals, so we drove Rebecca to my sister's house and went on to the hospital. As I was being admitted, Mark came running in, reeking of alcohol. My nosey neighbor had called him at the VFW to let him know there was a baby on the way.

My friend, Joan Cutwright and my mother were with me throughout that laborious day, for which I was grateful. Joan rubbed by feet and encouraged me to walk the floor, also to squat and push...as Native American women had done. I don't think it helped, but I loved having her support.

At around 9:00 or 10:00 that night I had had ENOUGH! So, a nurse came in and broke my water. I knew my doctor was nearly as anxious as I to get this over with. Earlier in the evening she informed me that she had out of town guests and wanted to get home as quickly as possible. An odd thing to say, I thought, to someone in my situation.

Soon I had dilated 10 cm and they were rushing me into the delivery room. By this time everyone was getting used to Greta and me having babies, so the place was not crawling with family members.

I wanted to be fully conscious for this birth, so opted out of anesthesia. There were no epidurals during labor in those days. We felt every ounce of our pain, with anesthesia only administered at the very last, if requested. I didn't want to miss one second of the miracle that was playing out before me.

It was not an easy birth. He got stuck in the birth canal as I pushed, and Dr. Cruz pulled. Finally, she made a large episiotomy and out come all 9 pounds 6 ounces and 22 inches of boy! He had a large head, broad shoulders and a terrible frown on his wrinkled face. He cried like a little squealing pig.

We had already named him Neil Andrew and I began laughing and calling him "Squealy Neily". He was slick and purple and beautiful, with a face like his sister's when she was born...and he was angry...with fists clenched and terrible cries. Who could blame him? Birth had been hard on us both.

As a nurse laid him on a scale, the doctor and anesthesiologist began betting on his weight. I was glad when the latter won guessing correctly to the ounce. I liked him. During those last grueling minutes of delivery, he had stroked my hair and spoken soft, encouraging words to me. How I longed for such a man in my life to help and comfort me during such challenging times.

While Dr. Cruz stitched me up, I rubbed Neil all over and put him to my breast and he latched on immediately. But I was exhausted, and he was jaundiced, so they whisked him off to the nursery. My baby was here...healthy and strong and full of attitude. I couldn't have been happier.

They tucked me into bed with ice on my sagging tummy and hot blankets swaddled around me up to my chin...turned on the TV and left me alone to process the amazing thing that had just occurred. Saturday Night Live was on and Steve Martin was being ridiculously funny. I started laughing...then crying...then laughing. I guess I was a little hysterical.

Next morning, they brought him to me. This huge baby boy had been squeezed into a tiny t-shirt that said, "Love made Visible at Greene County Memorial Hospital" on the front. I still have that little shirt. I talked, sang and laughed at all his funny expressions...something he continued, and earned the nick name "Little Clown" from his sister, who adored him. He was mildly interested in me, but when his father entered the room and said, "Hello son!" Neil knew him instantly and started craning his neck and struggling to open his swollen eyes to see him.

I realized then the vital role a man plays in his son's life...and I was sad for Neil because of this. I wanted so much for him to have a good role model, but there was none to be found...I allowed Mark to come back home.

I worked hard to be a good mother...it was my full occupation and my joy. But life wasn't easy for any of us. Alcoholism and rage were the order of the day and I was depressed much of the time, constantly fighting poverty and the indignities heaped upon me and my children. Later, when the kids were much older, I made decisions that didn't serve us well, and I have regrets.

Several years ago, Mark died of Huntington's disease, a neurological disorder of epic proportions. This may have contributed, I realize, to his impulse control issues...and I forgive him.

Despite all the challenges, Neil became a strong, resilient, industrious, self-made man. Against almost insurmountable odds, he conquered demons in the way, and built a meaningful life, brick by brick. He is the owner of a successful hardwood flooring company in Winston-Salem, NC and an amazingly kind and attentive father to our beloved Cora. She and her beautiful mother, Stephanie, love him dearly.

So do I. I am very proud to call Neil Andrew Rush, my son.

The name "Neil" means "Champion".

That he is.

NEIL

He is the wind...
A wild steed on the run-
Hooves beating the ground,
A terrible sound...
Going where?
His power will take him there,
Vibrating the air.

He's a dark wave pounding the shore...
A sunken ship on the ocean floor,
Where treasures abide and forever hide...
Too risky to find, but you know they're there...
It isn't fair.

He is the moon when a cloud passes 'oer
Casting light and shadow on earth's twilight floor-
Always leaving you grasping for more.

He is the moon, and the wind and the sun,
A vast ocean rolling,
A steed on the run...
He is my champion,
He is my son.

I Love You...
Mom

Update:

On the night of August 20th, 2019, my son...my baby... Neil Andrew Rush, was called to rest doing what he loved...riding his recreational vehicle near his home in Winston-Salem, North Carolina, leaving behind his devoted life partner, Stephanie, and beloved 5-year-old daughter Cora, who was his life and inspiration.

We are heart broken.
Goodbye, Cowboy.

Neil, Cora & Stephanie on Cora's
preschool graduation day.

Breathe life into this feeble heart.
Lift this mortal veil of fear.
Take these crumbled hopes, etched with tears.
We'll rise above these earthly cares.

Cast your eyes on the ocean.
Cast your soul to the sea.
When the dark night seems endless.
Please, remember me...
Please, remember me...

Loreena Mckennitt
From Dante's Prayer

REMEMBERING NEIL

My son is dead.

He is dead.

He is still dead.

I will tell you this. The first three months were paralyzing. You think you will die. You wish you would. Staying clean and fed becomes all you can manage, and just barely. Thank goodness for canned soup and yogurt.

The waves of grief take you under. Over and over, and over again.

Later, months later, the immensity of the shock of loss subsides somewhat. Some days you can breathe...feel without pain...see in color.

In June of 2019, his beloved daughter, Cora, graduated from preschool. Neil was nearly late for that event, after working a long day. He showered, sped to the venue, parked illegally, and ran in the rain, soaking his dress shirt and tie. He made it on time, breathless and smiling, just as proudly as he would had she been a young woman receiving her PhD...a dozen pink roses in hand.

Neil never raised his voice or displayed impatience with Cora. If she interrupted an adult conversation, rather than silencing her, he would pause the conversation with his signature, "What is it, baby?" Then hang onto her every word. She was his everything.

He bought an impressive home that he could scarcely afford, then spent the last two years of his life working night and day, quite literally, creating a beautiful homestead for his family. It wasn't unusual for Stephanie to fall asleep late at night, the sound of his tractor rounding the corner of the house, as he uprooted trees, dug up stumps, and rerouted a creek to keep it from flooding the bottom of the land.

One night, he drove me around his property on the Polaris Ranger, proudly showing me all of his finished and unfinished projects. I hated that ride. It was cold, and past Cora's bedtime...he seemed to be trying to scare me, as he climbed steep hills or drove sideways on embankments.

"These things were made for this," he explained. "The Ranger is an amazing machine."

I'm so glad we took that ride, and that I pretended to enjoy it: two months later, he died, doing the thing that he loved...riding that damn Ranger alone, at night, in a construction site.

It happened fast; we believe.

Life will never be the same.

The totality of child loss...no matter the age...with all its secondary losses, will morph, evolve, and change over time. But the constant feature. The undertow that never stops tugging at your heart; this unrelenting sorrow, will lighten in time.

And what you have left once you realize it's not going to kill you, is your unending love for them. And a raw determination to keep their memory alive, somehow. Even if it fades in every other person, as the smell of them fades on the clothes you can never get rid of.

I am Neil's mother. That's who I am.

And I am here to tell you that he lived. Not an easy, tidy, perfect life. It was messy and edgy and tragic. And fun and funny and fascinating, and big and rowdy and brave, and worthy of being remembered.

Please...please...please.

Never forget that.

Is he in God's memory, too? I hope so. Because any place is bound to be more interesting with him in it.

I love you forever, baby boy.

Mom.

ONE LAST DAY

How would I spend one last day with my son?

We would come together at his "homestead" for a meal. He would cook and Rebecca and I would assist him. He loved to cook. We would all be together again under the roof he loved with the people he loved...

Stephanie, Cora, Rebecca, Daniel and Owen. We would listen with all of our hearts to his long narratives...eat his food one last time, laugh, cry and hold onto one another.

He would say, "Y'all need to lighten up."

I would give anything...

NANCY INGRID HURD

"Shower the people you love with love,
Show them the way that you feel.
Things are going to be much better...
If you only will."

James Taylor

NANCY INGRID HURD

NEMACOLIN

In 1982 we moved to a small coal mining community in South Western PA...most of the older residents were direct descendants of European immigrants who had poured into the mining communities in PA and WV during the great immigrations of the early 20th century, to find work.

As must have long been the custom, every Monday morning and very early, these women would rush, as if in a marathon, to see who could get their laundry on the clothes lines first. I half-heartedly took part in this contest, knowing that I couldn't possibly compete. I would hear the two women on either side of my house bantering back and forth to each other across the yards, in their still recognizable hints of European accents.

"Nancy," I heard one say to the other indulgently, late one Monday morning when my laundry was still not on the line, her own gleaming white sheets dancing in the wind, "she's a good girl. And she's busy with a baby...we can't expect much from her."

Nancy
February 2017

DANCING ON BROKEN GLASS

In the winter of 1983, we moved to Phoenix, Arizona. It was an ill-fated and chaotic journey, the high points being a trip through the Sierra Nevada Mountains, and a wonderful visit to Santa Cruz, California. The rest I prefer to forget. Six months later, we moved back East and landed in the beautiful Blue Ridge Mountains and foothills of Western North Carolina, and I have not budged from here since. Nor do I intend to.

Roseanne, my sister-in-law at the time, was a troubled woman. She lived in a run-down old trailer in Hickory, NC with her second husband and six kids from her first marriage. The place was filthy! My husband, two children and I stayed with them for 3 weeks while he looked for work. Appalled by the conditions under which she was raising her family, I began to clean...and clean and cook... and clean some more. It was the only way I could let my kids stay there. Plus, I wanted however briefly, to make a difference in the lives of those children.

Roseanne's youngest daughter was memorable. She was bright spirited, lively and smiled readily form her exuberant heart.

One afternoon this child, all decked out in "dress-up" clothes...her mother's old skirt sweeping around her ankles, and a bonnet I had purchased for her at the flea market, took my daughter and me by the hands and lead us to the back of the trailer. "This is where I come to play", she said proudly, "It's not really a secret, but I can be alone here." It was the burned-out shell of a room. Charred boards and furniture lay in a heap on the blackened floor, which was covered in broken glass. I warned her that it was too dangerous to enter. "Oh no," she said letting go of my hand, "I come here all the time."

Then she did the most precious thing...with a shock of natural curls falling around that sweet, pale face...she started to dance. Twirling and swaying around that rancid room, oblivious to her pitiful surroundings, her eyes filled with profound joy. This child, who lived in chaos with her mother, five wounded siblings and a stepfather, who later served time for abusing her in ways I never would imagine...was happy.

I want to be like that. I want to find that beautiful place inside myself, where no injury can do lasting harm.

That resilient spirit eventually propelled her into a meaningful and abundant life...happily, all of her siblings have done well!

Sometimes, when my life feels unmanageable, I go back in my mind to that burned-out room in an old trailer in the foothills of North Carolina and try to remember what Adelle knew...that you can always choose to dance. Even if the floor is covered in broken glass.

Nancy
2014

CAREER PATH

After Mark and I separated, I found myself in much need of employment. I had only completed one year of college and other than homemaking, had no marketable skills. I had done much research in the area of natural healing over the years, so was happy to learn that a respected chiropractor in our town was looking for a therapist and room to room assistant.

I applied, was interviewed and was thrilled when Dr. Holloway's office manager, an impressive and imposing woman name Joyce Clydesdale, called to tell me I had gotten the position. I thrived in my new career. I spent the next 20 years of my life delving deeply into the field of holistic and alternative health care. I became licensed as a massage and body work therapist, colon hydrotherapist and was given the freedom to practice my craft with the confidence of one who has become proficient.

You must understand...up to this point I had lived in a war zone of indignities and deficiencies. Now I could care for the needs of my children without walking over landmines in the process. Mark had been a notorious tight wad. This new occupation, although not terribly lucrative, was like moving into a new dimension of healing and light. I was in my element.

One afternoon, a very debilitated woman entered our office. By this time, I was working for Dr. Holloway's sister, Sylvia, also a chiropractor and my friend. The poor dear was in great need of care. Often, we saw desperate people who had gone the allopathic medical route, found no relief and made their way to us as a desperate last resort.

This woman had been suffering from severe pain, abdominal swelling and nausea and had seen one of our local surgeons, who removed her gall bladder...yet the pain persisted. Over and over again she returned to him, but he insisted that she was still recovering from surgery, prescribed a round of antibiotics and sent her home.

When she came to us, I could see that this emaciated, suffering soul was very sick indeed. We did what we could for her. Gentle massage and spinal manipulation and a warm colonic. Our Reflexologist rubbed her feet until she fell into the first real sleep she had had in days. Although happy to bring her some comfort, it was clear that more was needed and quickly.

I got the idea to take an x-ray of her abdomen. This may seem like the obvious to you, but remember she was under the care of a reputable doctor, who insisted that nothing was seriously wrong. Also, x-rays ordinarily show up hard tissue anomalies. For soft tissue diagnostics you need ultrasound, CT or MRI scans.

But following my instincts in a sort of desperation, I did a film of her abdomen and found a shocking mass of small, white circles. Some regular, some irregularly shaped, throughout her lower left abdomen.

I showed the x-rays to Dr. Sylvia, who gave this lady the films and advised her to go immediately to any doctor in town, other than the one who had diagnosed her with gall stones. We never saw her again...but several weeks later received a letter in the mail from her husband, saying how much he appreciated our diligence and care. Tragically, his wife had been diagnosed with advance stage ovarian cancer and had passed away several days earlier, surrounded by everyone she loved.

The surgeon in question soon left town, I was later informed, having lost his reputation over this incident. I hope someone tarred and feathered him, first.

Every day I was happy to get up and go to work, knowing most days I was instrumental in helping to relieve the pain of another...though not terribly lucrative, it was rewarding and that was enough.

Sadly, it came to an end in 2008 when I developed a UPJ obstruction of the left ureter, making drainage from that kidney difficult. Over the years since then I have had two balloon procedures to try and open the obstructed area, which has been somewhat helpful...and four ureteral stents. Unfortunately, during this episode, I developed cipro toxicity, the antibiotic often prescribed for kidney issues and have permanent neurological and vestibular system damage as a result.

If you take nothing else away from my story, please beware of the fluoroquinolone class of antibiotics, and the suffering they have caused to thousands of people. Fluoroquinolones are actually a chemotherapeutic agent and cause mitochondrial or DNA damage. Thankfully, there is now a "black box" warning on these dangerous drugs...often the first step before removing a drug from the market.

But for me, the damage is done. I may look okay, but the invisible illness is very real. If you don't believe me, try walking a mile in my shoes sometime. It would give me a much-needed break. But believe me...after a few steps you will want to turn back.

I look with gratitude on the years I spent in the holistic health field and appreciate the valuable knowledge received working in close proximity with three excellent physicians...Walter and Sylvia Holloway, (sadly Sylvia is now deceased) and Dr. R. Ernest Cohn, MD/ND of the Holistic Medical Clinic of the Carolinas. His work was widely acclaimed by international health guru George Malcamus of "Hallelujah Acres" and referred to in some of Suzanne Somers books on health and wellness. I occasionally clashed with Dr. Cohn on matters of ethics, but he was the most gifted diagnostician I have ever known.

Shana

SHANA

We seldom talk about it, but we never forget. My pain is incidental here...this loss belongs to my sister, her husband and her daughters. I have watched them face it with strength and courage. I am proud to be a part of this family. I am Aunt Nancy, and I need to tell my recollections of events on that fateful day all those years ago.

It's time for someone to tell this story...December 13th, 1997. I awoke from a disturbing dream. Soon Neil, my sixteen-year-old son, entered the room to inform me that he and his cousin Sara were going hiking at "Stone Mountain" that afternoon. I knew that the terrain there was risky in places and people had been injured.

But Neil was a big, strapping boy...already over six feet tall and Sara was a young woman of eighteen. I wouldn't try to veto their plans. I had to be someplace that afternoon, I don't remember where, but on my way out the door Neil told me that Sara's younger sister, Shana and their friend Carrie would be joining them. Again, I felt concerned but said, "Have a good time. Be careful and come home before dark."

When I returned home later that evening, the phone was ringing as I walked through the door. It was my mother calling form PA, "Nan," she said, "I just heard from Greta and she said Shana was in an accident on Stone Mountain today. She didn't think it was too serious but she's on the way to the hospital. Could you run over and check on her, and then call to let me know how she is?"

I didn't feel terribly concerned...a sprained ankle maybe...a minor fracture. I combed my hair, threw on a sweater and headed out the door. When I got to the hospital a helicopter was landing on the front lawn. Somehow, I knew...it had come for Shana... Fear swept over me as I ran through sliding doors into the ER. First thing I saw was my brother-in-law, David, talking on the phone in the waiting room. "Bob", I heard him say to his friend..." It's really bad. We need you man...can you get over here?" "How is she?" I asked. He just shook his head.

Suddenly a doctor hurried in and asked for the "Rush" family. Greta and Sara were already on their way driving to Baptist Trauma Unit in Winston-Salem, NC. Dave had stayed behind with Shana until they got her onto the Life Flight.

I accompanied him, the doctor and a young nurse into a small room where a set of x-rays and CT scan were hurriedly placed on a lighted screen. Shana, the doctor explained, had fractured her skull at the brain stem. Chances of survival were very slim; I remember sliding out of a chair onto the floor and squeezing the nurse's hand so hard it hurt her.

I went to Dave and we hugged and cried. I felt so sad for him and my heart was breaking for my sister. Suddenly a nurse hurried us out and down the hall. Shana was lying on a stretcher by an open door, about to be boarded on the helicopter. She was lying there beautiful, with wisps of long red hair around her quiet face. There was no sign of pain anywhere. She was just sleeping.

I took her hand and told her that I loved her. A nurse placed Shana's jewelry in my other hand...then they whisked her away. I wanted so much to spend more time with her. But there was no more time.

Soon, my daughter Rebecca came, and Neil was with her. I knew how badly he must be hurting and put my arms around him. But he was a teen-aged boy...full of bravado and didn't want me to fuss over him. Especially when he needed it the most.

So, we made our long, unfamiliar journey to the hospital, getting lost on the way. I remember stopping at a gift shop that had just closed for the day, to ask for directions. I looked through the glass and saw two ladies chatting over the cash register. I banged on the door, but no one came, so I knocked again, harder, when a distraught looking woman answered. I told her our predicament and her face softened. "Follow me," she said. "I'll take you right over there." I appreciate her kindness more than I can say.

I was shaking as we entered the waiting area...my eyes scanning the room for my sister. I ran to her and hugged her close, waiting for the awful, inevitable news...but what she said gave me a glimmer of hope. Shana was still alive, and they were running some scans. There was still a chance, however small, that she might come through this. I told Greta how sorry I was for coming late, explaining that we had gotten lost on the way.

Greta was in shock. "Time," she said...her eyes wandering, "it means nothing to me now..." My attention went to Sara. She was driving at the time of the accident. How must she be feeling?

The girls needed a restroom before starting out on their hike that afternoon, which was down a little gravel road...so Sara jumped into the driver's seat, Neil took his place on the passenger side, then Shana and Carrie jumped up onto the back end of the car.

They rode this way very slowly down to the paved parking lot when Shana either jumped or fell off the car...feet first, then her bottom, then her head hit the blacktop. She went unconscious immediately. "Wake up Shana!" the kids teased..." time to get up!" "Shana's dead," one of them said jokingly. They thought she was pretending. Then she started turning blue, Neil ran for help; soon a ranger came, and an ambulance was called...

...and now here we all were at Baptist Trauma Center waiting for a word...praying for a good outcome...fearing the worst.

Mary, one of Greta's older daughters arrived from Asheville with her new husband. As long as I live, I will never forget the sound of that poor girl crying...wailing...over her sister. Oh, Mary...I am so sorry.

There was a long hallway encircling the waiting area with a handrail around it. I saw Sara, all alone, pacing up and down the hallway hand over hand along the rail, her long hair spilling down her back. She looked lost, frightened, angry.

"I should have stopped her" she said, "I was the oldest, and I should have stopped her." I told her it could have happened to anyone. "It's not your fault," I assured her. "Shana had a mind of her own, and a strong one. You couldn't have stopped her. It seemed like harmless fun; kids do this kind of thing all the time. I've done it! Usually with no consequence at all. But please don't despair. She may recover from this."

Sara looked me square in the face..." No," she said, "she won't. She's going to die."

My heart ached for Sara. Clearly, it was not her fault. They were children and they were playing, doing what kids do, enjoying life, testing the limits.

It was simply no one's fault. And no one has thought otherwise for one second.

After what seemed like an eternity of waiting, the family was called back to a consultation room. The doctor was kind. He said that if she could hang on for the next few hours, there was still a chance that she could make it...but the scans did not look good.

We all grabbed ahold of that shining little glimmer of hope and clung tightly to it. "Can I sit with her?" my sister asked, "Of course" he answered. "A nurse will come for you soon and take you back."

So, when the nurse came and called for the immediate family, we didn't think much about it. After what seemed like forever, I looked down the hall and saw them all returning, and Dave was pushing Greta in a wheelchair. The girls were crying and holding onto each other.

I could see it in their faces...the worst had happened. Shana was dead. I can't even begin to imagine what they went through that night...those last terrible, precious moments with their youngest daughter and little sister.

Unplugging machines, saying good-bye to that lovely, lively flame. Shana, the noisy, happy, exuberant one, was gone. She was only fifteen years old.

It was now our turn to say good-bye and my children and I started down that long corridor. Rebecca held my hand...I could scarcely walk...but I made myself go in. She was so pale...so still, with her long red hair spread over the pillow. Oh, Shana! I couldn't go to her.

Our friend came in behind us. "Bob," I said, "please cut a lock of her hair for Greta." Dave had returned. "No," he said, "don't do that." I became more insistent. "If it were Rebecca, I would want a lock of hair. You cut my sister a lock of her baby's hair!" Dave conceded and Bob cut a bit of that beautiful hair for Greta.

I had to be wheeled back to the waiting room where someone parked me beside my sister. We held hands. Everyone was in shock by this time.

At some point, it all blurs in my memory now, we all ended up in the home of Alexus, Greta's oldest daughter, who lived in Winston-Salem. Friends began to file in bringing food, wine, making coffee.

My mother was on her way from Pennsylvania with our friends, Jamey and Maggie. Seven hours she was in that car not knowing what she would find when they arrived. Maggie kept Mom busy playing trivia and word games. I drove back to the hospital to meet them and break the awful news to my mother.

How I dreaded it...Shana adored her Grandma, "Gahgoo" and paid special attention to her...visiting her often, writing frequent cards, letters and funny little stories. They had a special bond and my heart ached for her.

It was after 2:00 a.m. when they arrived. I ran to Mom, putting my arms around her and saying as gently as I could, "Our little girl is gone." She was in shock by the time we got back to Alexus' house...I guess we all were.

Alexus, Mary and their husbands, Rebecca and Sara had retired to the upstairs bedroom. Six young adults-all shattered-lying together in one bed for what remained of the night. I heard

153

them through the hours, talking in hushed tones...laughing...crying...taking comfort in one another, as each tried to come to terms with the totality of their loss.

Neil on the other hand, took a sleeping bag into a back room and shut the door behind him. I encouraged him to go be with the other young people or downstairs with me and Gahgoo, but he wanted to be alone. I left him there in the darkness with his solitary pain...concerned that he would stay too isolated and grieve in ways that could be harmful to him; (and that is another story).

He and Shana had been close friends for all of his life. She helped him with homework, laughed at him, teased him, (good naturedly) and always urged him on to reach higher. He was devastated by her death.

My mother and I slept on opposite ends of the sofa that night. "Are you alright?" I kept asking, "Yes...are you?" We both lied. "I'm so glad Shana doesn't know what happened," she said. "She would just hate to be dead."

The first thing I heard in the morning was David, back in the master bedroom, crying like his heart would break. "Little girl...little girl..." he kept saying, and Greta's voice, quiet and comforting.

They pulled together through his terrible tragedy-drawing strength from each other and their incredible faith, which fortified and sustained them. They are wonderful. They are my Heroes.

The days, months and years have passed since that awful night...Shana is a memory now, strong and light as a beacon in a dark sea. I hoped that I would never forget the sound of her laughter, and I haven't. I can draw it up out of the well of my memory at any given moment and hear it again, like yesterday...rich and glorious through the passing years.

This is my story. My sister and her family each have their own version of the events of that night...their loss born privately in the recesses of each heart.

They have walked through the valley of the shadow and come out on the other side. They take comfort in the Bible's promise of a resurrection and just see her in that place where *"death will be no more...neither will mourning, nor outcry, nor pain be anymore. The former things have passed away."* (Rev. 21:3,4)

Shana...I often wonder where life would have taken you. Where would you be today? A wife? A mother? How would you look as a woman? You just left us too soon.

But we hold on to this hope. We want to see you again. Of course, it will take a miracle. But is resurrection any more or less miraculous than birth? I think not. He can do this...this restoration of humankind. He has done greater things than this.

So, until that time of reunion, rest in peace, sweet girl.

Aunt Nancy
2015

NANCY INGRID HURD

NEIL & SHANA
Surviving the Deaths of Our Children

When I was a girl in Grant Town, WV, we were friends with a wonderful family who lived nearby. Several years ago, while visiting my grandfather in that town, I stopped in to see Mrs. B.

I remember very well as a child staring at a picture on the wall above their stairway; of a handsome little boy, her son, who had died at only 12 years of age. The gravity of their loss affected me even then, though I had never met him.

The day I stopped by to visit, the subject of child loss came up, since my sister had recently lost her beautiful daughter, Shana. I have never forgotten what Mrs. B. said to me that day.

After the death of her son she had gone into a terrible depression, she couldn't sleep, could barely eat and the work of caring for her remaining family nearly ceased. This went on for many weeks. Then one day she took a good look at her situation, thought of her husband and 3 daughters, and said, "Life is for the living".

She got up, cleaned up, went downstairs and resumed the care of her family.

Her words stuck with me through the years and have taken on new meaning since the recent death of my son. Many times a day I repeat those words out loud or silently..." Life is for the living".

The pain is always beneath the surface. Sometimes it comes up in smothering waves. But I have other family...my mother, my daughter, my grandchildren...and they need me.

I am not walking this road alone, others have paved the way for me, and I humbly walk in their courageous footsteps.

When the very worst thing that can happen to a parent happens, what is left??

Life. And it is for the living.

"I wish people would understand that grief lasts forever because love lasts forever. That the loss of a child is not one finite event, it is a continuous loss that unfolds minute by minute, over the course of a lifetime. Every "should be" milestone we miss...back to school years and graduations; weddings that will never be; grandchildren that should have but will never be born...an entire generation of people are irrevocably lost forever. That is why grief lasts forever. The ripple effect never ends...the bleeding never stops."

Angela Miller
(from "A Bed for My Heart")

Gary & Nancy
June 2, 1998

I was standing at a precipice
Silent and alone-
Searching the horizon
For a place to call my home.
The cold dark clouds of yesterday
Still lingered near behind,
But a soft warm wind is blowing now
Erasing them from mind.
I see you in the distance and
Sensing that you care,
Traverse the miles in seconds...
As in dreams...to reach you there.
My friend...we have been scarred
By life in spirit, shall we dress
Each other's wounds with kindness?
Pour on the oil of tenderness?
Then together walk the rough terrain,
Until we reach the land,
Where broken dreams are swept away
By a loving Father's hand.

Love,
Nancy

THE INVITATION

It was a beautiful card. All the cards he sent her were beautiful...fine and elegant, "for those who care to send the very best."

The message was simple and compelling..." Dear Eliza, if possible, I would like to meet with you on our anniversary, Saturday June 2nd. Will you have dinner with me? Sixth and Main or Angelica's...your choice. There is something special I wish to give you in person. I do pray that you are continuing to improve each day...Love, Paul"

No one in her family or circle of friends had expressed concern over her marriage to Paul nine years earlier. She had avoided all of that by marrying him quickly and secretly.

Looking back, she knew it had been an impulsive and selfish act. Impulsive because she barely knew him. Selfish, because she had two nearly grown children who had met him only once and very briefly. "Who was that woman?" she had asked herself a million times since that fair June day in 1998 when she walked with Paul and two of his friends into the courthouse in Boone, North Carolina and recited marriage vows to a stranger.

Who was she, indeed? How had it happened? Something more mysterious than her value system and better judgement had compelled her on that day. Perhaps she had been overtaken by her history of low self-esteem and abusive relationships. I don't claim to know what motivates Eliza...I am merely reporting.

But he was a beautiful man. They often remarked later that their attraction had been at the cellular level...and so it must have been...for they were drawn inexplicably and deeply to each other from that first meeting in Dr. Fritz's office.

When he shook her hand, his hand felt like her own. He was a small man, strong built and muscular, but delicate too...with olive skin and shoulder length salt and pepper hair, penetrating dark eyes and lovely smile. He stood there in jeans and berks, looking at her like he'd always known her. Dr. Fritz had introduced them. He was an old naturopath in the Blue Ridge Mountains and Eliza's employer. He and his dingy wife Doreen thought that they would be a good match.

Bingo, Dr. Fritz and Doreen.

That first meeting was soon followed by a luncheon date, then dinner, then a walk on the Greenway Trail and more dinners...culminating in a bond so deep that in only two months' time they were pledging their undying love as they clung to each other, weeping years of pent up pain.

Their love was indisputable, though it seemed so strange looking back-that the bond had not broken. The tie that nearly destroyed Eliza's physical and mental health never diminished. So why...after all that had happened between them, could she not stop loving him?

Why the years of separation had not made her forget? Because she's stupid, that's why...or perhaps there is a better explanation. The truth of the matter was...he adored her. I mean really adored her. If her socks matched, he acted like she had come upon a spark of genius.

He found her funny and smart and beautiful, so when they were together, she felt smart, funny and beautiful. He was the man who opened car doors and pulled the seat belt around her. He was the man who not only put her needs before his own, but actually anticipated her needs.

She wanted for nothing. He was quite devoted to making her life happy and comfortable. Often, he asked, "Do you feels safe and loved?" How she felt meant something to him...and she adored him. She loved his sensitivity and humor...his smile...his touch...even the way he smelled...like an organic garden or rainwater in a barrel.

And his tastes were refined. They loved the same books, music and movies. Theirs was, as Paul would say, "A deep and abiding love." ...and it was.

She couldn't remember how soon after marrying him that the abuse began. All she could recall was that one morning her wonderful Paul walked out the door, and that evening another man walked in. It dazed and devastated her.

His eyes intense and darting about the room...he was demanding, critical, cynical. He began by quietly backing her into a corner, literally and figuratively. Demanding, demeaning, menacing...there was no way to talk her way out of his interrogations. They were designed to trap her...leaving her without defense or hope of peace and reconciliation.

Then the rage would begin. The screaming...more insane allegations...until finally, exhausted, he would recede into the bedroom where he would stay often for days, with his back to her...silent, cold and brooding. Sometimes the stone walling lasting for weeks. She had no defense against him during these turbulent times-so she, defeated, frightened and fragile, would leave...escaping to a friend or family member until the storm had passed.

Then she would return to the man who waited for her...apologetic, kind, penitent. It would never happen again, he promised through tears. Relieved to be home, she would acquiesce. And their delightful life would begin again...until the next time.

Finally, after four years, sick and broken, Eliza left for good...or evil...she could never decide. All she knew was she couldn't live with the man she loved. Or without him.

So, when she received "The Invitation", with great heaviness of heart she answered simply, "Dear Paul...I am not well and don't have the strength to see you at this time. Please know that you are in every thought and prayer. I hope you're well...Love, Eliza"

She knew he would contact her again; he always did. And that she would see him again. She couldn't stop, she couldn't find closure.

P.S.

Fast forward 11 years. Today she is finding closure and understanding. In abusive relationships, "trauma bonding", as well as addiction to dramatic emotional ups and downs, is a real thing. The attraction between "cluster B" personality disordered people and co-dependents, is undeniably strong.

Eventually, someone just has to stop the dance. Finally, that is what Paul and Eliza did. Their divorce was final two weeks ago (December 2018).

Sunday Ride

He would come by to get me
And off we would go
For a long Sunday drive
With his dog in tow.
And into the fire
Of a red sunset
We stirred up ashes
Of desire and regret.
Memories came
That I pushed far away...
The last thing I wanted
Was to love him today.
I must keep it simple.
It's only a ride.
Just a truck and a man
With a dog by his side.
All of these feelings in time
will subside...
For a man with a truck
And a dog in tow.
How he broke my heart
He'll never know.

NH
2019

NANCY INGRID HURD

THE DREAM

I slept peacefully last night...dreamed lavishly.

A little African American girl...chubby and sweet, sat on the sun splashed floor of this room, staring at a small unidentifiable black object. I was amazed by her ability to focus...she was just a baby.

After a long time, a pretty woman...very natural looking, came looking for the child. I told her how good her baby had been. She was a bit stand-offish, but pleasant. She gathered the child up in her arms and left the room.

I glanced at the bed across from mine and someone was sleeping there. She was small...undressed, lying on her stomach with long, blonde hair spilling out around her. I realized that it was me as a young woman. I slipped over and touched her arm trying to communicate...I don't know...something.

Suddenly I felt myself split and I was that woman...as well as who I am today. In an instant the woman became a child. "Little Nancy," with whom I've been struggling with for most of my life. She was sleeping. I put my arms around her and felt this wonderful integration...then my dream ended.

(January 2003, from a Women's Shelter in Wilkesboro NC)

NANCY INGRID HURD

INTROSPECTION

March 17, 2005

I have to ask myself...do I deserve light? Do I deserve heat? Adequate amounts of rest...the right kinds of food? Do I deserve kindness? Fairness? The correct compensation for work done? A cup of tea with lemon...the time it takes to boil the water? The time it takes to drink it?

How about friendship...relationships with people whom I choose, not just those who thrust their way into my life, or side wind in like a snake when I'm sick and lonely...poor and desperate. Am I worth the effort involved in learning a new skill? The money it costs to heal me when I'm sick? Flowers, pretty clothes, pleasant...even beautiful surroundings? Am I worth getting to know...do I possess anything of value you might want or need?

Worth the privilege of being selective about who or what I bring into my life, or home or heart? Am I worthy of setting boundaries for myself...of having those boundaries respected? Do I have the right to say no...anytime...for any reason...or for no apparent reason other than, "this is my space and I require privacy right now?"

Am I finally old enough to have a little peace and quiet...do I deserve that? ...And, what about love-even on days when I feel unlovable, unworthy and undeserving.

May I have compassion...tenderness...passion...understanding, without having to jump through impossible hoops? Can I love in return-without desperation, without fear...without the destruction of myself? I think so.

At least I am finally beginning to think so.

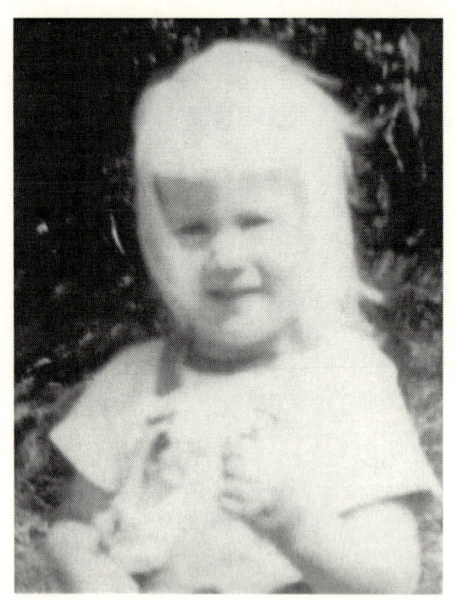

THE WINTER OF MARIE BLACKBURN

I meant, this time, not to get involved with my neighbors. My move to Blowing Rock, an artsy resort town in the mountains of Western North Carolina last month, was a soft landing for me...and one that I scarcely expected to happen given my physical and financial limitations. A kidney ailment and anxiety disorder have somewhat diminished my ability to be self-supporting.

Yet, here I am in this dear little town surrounded by ski slopes and gorgeous mountain vistas...rubbing elbows with artists, writers and vacationers from everywhere. Some afternoons I sit in the park and watch passers-by. I'm sure I look like a lonely old woman who ought to be feeding crumbs to pigeons. The variety of accents from around the country and even the world always impresses me.

I live in a small apartment complex on Canyon Street. If there was a slum in Blowing Rock, this would be it...but there are no slums in Blowing Rock. My apartment is lovely. I listen to soothing music, dine by candlelight...rest as needed. At night I leave my bedroom window slightly ajar and can hear the wind whistling around my building.

Sometimes, depending on the moon, I watch the silhouettes of pine trees swaying outside my window. If ever in my life I've felt contentment it is now. I love my solitude and fully intended to remain a stranger in this little town. Therefore, it was with hesitation that I answered a soft knock on my door two weeks ago.

There in the chilly evening air stood a slight-built elderly woman holding a paper plate in her hands. I accepted her gift of apple-cinnamon muffins, exchanged hurried introductions and offered her a seat in my living room; with the thought, "how do I get rid of her quickly without seeming impolite?"

In the course of our brief conversation, I learned that Marie is nearly blind. A victim of wet macular degeneration, (the worst kind) she sees only in vague outlines. She could not see my face...she cannot see her own face in the mirror...so I was impressed with how neat she was...her glossy white hair in a stylish cut...she appeared to be a woman who had been successful in life before misfortune changed her.

She had suffered a major stroke twenty years earlier but, through grueling therapy, had regained her ability to walk and speak...then to be stricken with blindness! I was amazed that Marie had found my door in the darkness. "Remember dear," she said, "I am always in darkness. I counted my steps here and I'll count them home again...I must maintain my independence" ...my respect for this woman was growing, so last night I decided to pay her a visit. Marie welcomed me with warmth and grace into her light, beautifully arranged home.

She had been an antique dealer for many years and her taste was exquisite. I helped her with a bit of paperwork she's no longer able to do for herself. Sitting across from her on the sofa I added some figures on a calculator. Marie wore a gray pantsuit, her white hair shining in the light of her immaculate living room. "Have you ever been married?" I asked casually, "do you have any children?" "Yes," she answered, "He was an alcoholic. We were married only a few short years. We had three children, but he didn't want to be a part of their lives. He died quite some time ago."

"How are your children now?" I asked...Marie hesitated. I glanced up from my calculations and saw tears in her eyes. I lay the calculator down and give her my full attention. Marie took a deep breath and began to tell me her story...

"Nancy," she said. "I'm in a bit of a predicament. The thing is...I didn't expect to live this long." She smiled and wiped away a tear. "My children," she continued, "want nothing to do with me." "How old are they?" I asked. "Cindy is forty-four, Michael, forty-two and Joey is forty...you see," she said, "they blame me for what happened to them. I did protect them once I knew what was happening...it's just that...for a long time I didn't know, and the damage had already been done."

I sat silent as Marie grappled with her pain. It was awhile before she spoke again..." I married Jim when the children were quite young. Back then you didn't hear much about abuse...and there wasn't much help for abused women. Divorce was not so common as it is today...it was such a disgrace, and I had been divorced once before, so I intended to stay with him and do my best. He never hit the children, but he nearly beat the life out of me. Some nights I'd wake up to a gun pointing at my head. He was mentally ill. I didn't know it when I married him...he seemed alright."

Again, Marie hesitated, fighting back tears. I wanted to reach out and take her hand, but it seemed to me that her struggle was a private one, so I sat still. I was riveted...my eyes focused on Marie's unseeing eyes...her pain was obvious. "My dear," she said quietly, "this isn't easy."

"Marie," I answered, "you don't have to do this. You really don't have to tell me anything."

She continued, "I've told this to no one in all these years, but" ...she confessed, "I was recently diagnosed with cancer. I'm choosing not to have treatment. I've been through radiation and chemotherapy before, and I just don't have the strength to go through that again. I am not asking for sympathy...I'm just reporting. I really am alright with it. However, one thing I must do before I die is tell somebody what happened to my children."

"Of course, Marie," I said, "if you need to talk...of course."

Marie continued..." One afternoon while I was at work my daughter, who was barely thirteen at the time, called and said that something was wrong with Joey. He was crying and was holding a sum of money and wouldn't tell her where he had gotten it.

"Instinctively I knew something was terribly wrong, so I quickly got a ride home and found Joey lying on the floor of his bedroom in the fetal position. He was crying inconsolably and had some money in his hand...he had been raped by his stepfather...the money given as a bribe not to tell. He was only nine years old."

Marie shifted uncomfortably in her seat, the rage in her face barely concealed. "I ran to my daughter who confided that she and Jim had been having relations for a long time and that he had threatened to kill her, her brothers and me, if she ever told. She was a prisoner of secrecy and isolation. The truth finally came spilling out as she confessed that Michael was also a victim. In that instant I decided to kill him. I would first take the children to our ministers' home on some pretext, then I would wait for Jim to return and I would kill him. I wanted him dead, and I wanted to be the one to pull the trigger...our house was an arsenal.

"He was a military man and owned several guns and loads of ammunition, but on this day, there was not a gun to be found. Inexplicably he had removed them all from our home. I went into Joey and said..." I promise you that I will never let him hurt you again. Do you trust Mommy?' "Yes," he said through tears. "Then dry your eyes. Go upstairs and wash your face in cold water. Children, we're going to play a game tonight. No one must say a word about any of this when Jim comes home. Tonight, I'm going to prepare a delicious dinner and we'll all sit down to eat as usual..."

When Jim came home that evening Marie had prepared a wonderful meal...Jim even complimented her on it. The family ate in silence without a hint that trouble was brewing just beneath the surface. Her broken heart and seething anger Marie kept hidden.

"Jim," she said later as she cleared the table, "Stan and Louise have had their new baby and were wondering if I might come over tonight and help out a little while." At his ease, Jim replied, "That was a fine dinner, Marie. I guess you can go."

The children were instructed in advance to speak up at this point...Marie said a silent prayer..." Can we go too?" they asked. "Please?" "We want to see the new baby...please?" Jim eyed his family suspiciously, then replied "Oh alright, go ahead. I guess you're all determined to leave me here with the dirty dishes tonight."

Marie thanked him, loaded her three battered children into the station wagon and drove straight to the police. Later that evening Jim was picked up. After a trial found him guilty of child molestation, he spent four and half years in prison and four years in a mental institution. The last thing he ever said to Marie was; "This is not over yet. I will find you...I will kill torture and kill your children in front of you, then I'll kill you."

There were few resources available to help Marie and her family get through this harrowing experience. Although she did get counseling for herself and the children, she also received some ostracism in the community and the minister of their church actually said, "Marie, how could you do this to him?"! They moved away...but the wounds in her now middle-aged children have never mended, as they struggle with drugs and alcohol addiction. They do not speak to their mother because, as they say, she married the man who ruined their lives.

When she finished, I sat in silence, feeling the despair of this dear lady who felt compelled to tell her tragic story to me, a stranger, before she died. "Thank you, Marie," I finally said, "You're a courageous woman. Maybe someday your children will get the healing they deserve and find a way to forgive you. You really did protect them with your life and someday they'll know that. I don't know what more you could have done."

Marie answered, "I don't have the advantage of reading faces anymore...but I do read voices...and yours is very kind. Thank you for listening. It was a hard story to tell, and I dare say a hard one to hear."

We said goodnight, and I headed up the sidewalk toward my apartment...my heart aching for Marie and her family. "Nancy," she called after me, "This Friday is the biggest shopping day of the year. Would you like to run into town awhile? I could use a new pair of black slacks...I've lost so much weight...and since I don't drive..."

"Of course," I said. "We'll go shop and maybe have a bit of lunch somewhere in town. I'll call you." ...so much for my decision not to get involved with neighbors...

...last night a chilling wind blew up from the North East. In my sleep I could hear it...like a child wailing...I awoke in a panic. I went into the kitchen to comfort myself with a cup of hot tea.

Pulling my robe tightly around me, I asked myself, who will care for this seemingly alone woman as her illness inevitably progresses? Who, I wondered, will be holding her hand when those vacant eyes close for the last time?

I don't have the answer to those questions. But let me tell you what I do know...Her apartment is only two doors down from mine....and tomorrow is Black Friday...and we're going shopping.

Nancy
November 26, 2009

TEA & CAKE, ANYONE?

This is a semi-long story, so skip now if you are in a hurry. On social media, I see post after post about gun control... and although politically neutral, understandably this is a hot topic.

So here is the story:

Pearl Buck's mother, (Peal Buck was the author of "*The Good Earth*", for those who may not know), and father were missionaries in China during the late 1800's. Pearl Buck was a child when the local people, half crazed by famine and hunger, decided that the famine was an indication that the gods were angry about there being "white devils" (Pearl Buck's family) in their midst. Her father was away on a journey when the local men decided that the time had come to kill the offending "white devils".

Her mother, except for her children and two servants, was alone in the house. She was defenseless. How would she protect her children from the heinous crime that the townsmen were determined to commit?

She had one weapon and one weapon only. Human kindness. As the men converged upon her home cursing and wielding clubs, she opened the doors wide, smiling, with her children freshly bathed and playing innocently upon the floor, the house smelling of tea cakes. She invited them in, two at a time, apologizing that she hadn't the room to seat them all together.

She gave them all hot tea and cake, chatting pleasantly in their language. The men sat and ate, staring at the floor, embarrassed by her unabashed kindness and ashamed of themselves as they ate her food and watched her children playing, then they all went quietly away.

That night Pearl Buck could hear her mother in her room, alone, crying.

It was years before she knew how much danger they had been in that night and how her mother's courage and kindness had saved them.

True, this story could have had a tragic ending. But she would have died doing the right thing, and that is not such a bad thing.

We may be armed to the teeth...but there will always be someone bigger, stronger and more heavily armed than we. At some point, the madness just has to end. Let it stop here.

Tea and cake, anyone?

DEBBIE

She was just the most insanely wonderful person I have ever known. So full of life, love and laughter...the essence of grace, good taste and good humor. Her entire being just screamed, "I am an amazing woman!"

And she was kind. And she was a great mother, a fabulous cook, an understanding friend, a caring daughter, an awesome wife.

I met Deb at another low ebb in my life...we had just made the trek across country from Arizona and I found myself a refugee of sorts in North Carolina, in much need of a friend. And, she wanted to be that for me. She wanted to be my friend.

This quality human being with a son the same age as mine, started arranging luncheons and play dates, taking me under her wing and into that big heart of hers. I doubted that I had much to give her in return. "A few lunches and girl talks will be nice", I thought, "until she gets to know the real me and thinks better of our friendship."

She so disagreed! She gave me confidence and assurance that I was...well...wonderful, because she believed that to be true about me and against all odds...in spite of many ups and downs in both our lives, she remained my truest and dearest friend for twenty-seven years, until her tragic death on March 20th, 2010.

My memories of Debbie are so expansive, they have become, in part, who I am. She is in the music I listen to, the books I read, the clothes I wear...the way I decorate. Such was her influence in my life. Often during the day, I still find myself saying, "I need to tell Debbie that."

So, you know what? I just do...I just tell her...because she is everywhere in my heart where anything beautiful still dares to grow...and the essence of her still lingers in that vast, unbelievable forever place where she still calls sometimes and says, "Well, hey, Nan! I just cooked (this or that) and it's delicious, and I was just wondering if you could come over!"

My fav Debbie quote....

"Nothin' like a wig and a set of false fingernails to make you feel like a REAL woman!"

Debbie

Debbie

To Debbie

Eyes like fireflies in the night
In her garden of delight
Laughter floating from her lips
Birds light upon her fingertips.

She lives in an enchanted land
Jewels sparkle on her hand
Children gather at her feet
Grown up ladies have a seat
For tea in painted china cups
To gossip over sips and sups.

She lives in an enchanted place
Dressed in yards of Spanish lace
Seasons changing in her face

How shall I describe my friend...?
The fairy princess of the glen
Sitting by an emerald pool
Where the air is still and cool...

"Come", she says, "And sit with me...
And all you have to do is be...
I love you just the way you are" ...
Then reaches for a glistening star
And lays it in your grateful hand
And you become a princess too...
It is the gift she gives to you...

She sees all that you can be
Then says it's what you've always been
But in your heart, you know what's true...
It is the gift she gives to you.

"What can I give you back?", I cry...
With a sparkle in her eye
And essences of truth and grace
Lighting up her lovely face...
Her voice fills with quiet love...
"What you've given is enough."

She lives in a fairy land
Giving from her gracious hand
She lives in a fairy fable
Giving from her bounteous table.

With Love from Nancy
© Copyright 1996 Nancy Hurd

My best friend of 27 years, Deborah Noblitt Church, 1954-2010.

IN LOVING MEMORY OF

Deborah Noblitt Church

Deborah Noblitt Church died on Saturday, 20 March, 2010, at 56 years old. She relished all things beautiful and good and had delighted in the warmth of that lovely nearly-spring day. Debbie's beloved husband of 36 happy years, Benny, and her cherished sons and granddaughter, Joshua, Micah and Alexa, will hold tightly to their many treasured memories of their special wife, mother, and grandmother. Deb's mother, Juanita Hicks of Albemarle, N.C., was seen by Deb as the standard of a loving wife to her husband, Jim, both of whom Deb deeply loved. She laughed with her adored brothers, Charlie Noblitt and John Noblitt, and who, with their families, were close to her heart. Wonderful times were enjoyed with her special uncle and aunt, Jim and Maria Noblitt, of Raleigh, N.C.

Many, many friends will mourn the loss of this delightful "bubble" who nicknamed herself Dakota Sunshine.

Deb was predeceased by her father, Charles Noblitt; her grandparents Perry E. and Dorsie Mae Ferguson, Charles G. and Bess Noblitt, and a special friend of the family, Mary Lou Robinson.

Saturday, 27 March, at 7:00 p.m., there will be a funeral service at the Wilkesboro, N.C., Kingdom Hall of Jehovah's Witnesses on 1515 River Street, Wilkesboro, N.C.

The Author

REFLECTIONS

I just moved through a three-month illness. Much of that time was spent in bed. Here's what I've learned...

We are not stronger in the broken places, but weaker. Like a cracked plate.

Your body is not as strong as you thought, so better start cultivating mind and spirit now.

Depression is self-limiting as a cold and will not kill you. It washes over you like a dark wave, does its dirty work, and washes away again... (until the next round) ...you can stand the pain.

On another note, I observed that birds are not as peaceful as they sound. They are very scrappy creatures, in a daily fight for survival. If you place a feeder in your yard, their true colors will emerge. Only Robin's won't take part in the fight; (probably because they are ground feeders), and I have a new respect for them.

Yesterday for the first time in weeks, I ran downstairs with a basket of laundry on my hip to wash clothes, whispering "thank you" under every grateful breath. What was once drudgery, became a joy, simply because I can do it again.

I look behind me over the last few months, (I know it sounds cliché), but I think I really am seeing footprints in the sand... ...and they're not mine.

2012

NANCY INGRID HURD

THE PACKAGE

Today I received a package in the mail from my Aunt Peggy. There were tea bags in bright wrappers...peppermint, ginger and Earl Grey...and photographs of my Grandmother's flower garden. I pictured myself a child again, sitting on the lowest porch step embraced by the smell of honey suckle and lavender with Aunt Peggy's youngest daughter beside me, laughing and waving away a persistent bee.

In the envelope she had tossed a handful of dried lavender. It spilled on the bed when I opened it. I love this Aunt. "You are," she writes to me, "as good as any angel..." and I begin to cry, tasting salty tears. I always cry when anyone says something kind to me.

She was a wife for over sixty years. She went, she tells me, to the Alzheimer's unit last week to visit him. It is many miles away. They are compassionate there, she says, and he gets good care. She thinks he recognizes her. She pushes him in his wheelchair up and down the halls. They stop to admire each painting they pass. Does he remember what kind of bird this is, or flower, she asks...mostly he does. Does he remember how unkind he had been?

I believe they both have forgotten that part.

She pushes him back into the dining room...this shadow of a man who fathered her six children and worked as hard as anyone ever has. This man through whom she had to learn the meaning of true forgiveness. She washes his hands and face and feeds him...it was a good day.

I am taken back once more to that bottom step, surrounded by my grandmother's flowers. I am waiting for him to come. It is the summer of my 3rd year and I have not yet learned that the family doesn't care for him. I haven't yet learned what this means...so my heart quickens when I see his station wagon pull up in front of my grandmother's house.

Up, up, up over his shoulder I go. "Ol' sack of feed." he says to me, laughing...we both laugh. I never tire of his attention.

...some bits of lavender have fallen to the floor. I pick up each fragrant, treasured piece; and brushing away a persistent tear, place them carefully back into the envelope...something to keep for the rest of my life...along with each treasured memory of my kindred spirit, lover of every living, growing, flying and creeping thing, Aunt Peggy.

She is as good as any angel.

Aunt Peg

NUANCE – LIGHT IN THE SHADOWS

noō͝ anˈs/noun
1.   "A subtle difference in shade of meaning or sound. Fine
distinction.

I seldom see anything simply in black and white. My
impressions of life, people and events are full of color..."
subtle differences in shades of meaning...fine distinction"
drawn from everyday occurrences.

The light on the corner of Sunset and Main does not simply
turn red. As it turns, the pretty girl in pink shorts takes
selfies...letting her friends know that she is HERE. In this
world...in this tourist town and will not be ignored. And an
elderly woman hobbles across on the arm of the old gentleman
whose devotion has not diminished with age and infirmity.
And my heart hurts...because I am here, too. And I want that
kind of love...

I have been hurt in this life. I feel it in body, mind and spirit.
However bruised and battered, I am strangely not bitter. I see
nuances of light and shadow in those with whom I have spent
my time or invited in to share my table or my bed.

Mark loved to dance. I never tired of watching him. He
moved across the floor like James Brown and 'any old music
would do'. Sometimes we danced in the kitchen. We would
kick off our shoes and slow dance, while he sang love songs...off
key... in my ear...a light in that troubled alliance. He stalked, he
berated, he pushed and violated...shadows in the light.

My children...his children, graced our lives and made it, every
bit of it...worthwhile. Light in the shadows.

My father...lying in a quiet room with mounds of home-made
quilts covering his cancer reduced body...I read him from the
23rd Psalm over and over, and he never tires of it. This proud
man, who in my life seldom said he loved me or showed
approval; so that I could not love or approve of myself,

showered me with words of endearment in his last days. I
couldn't get enough...my heart hungry for each "I love you,"
and "I am so proud of you," until all the years of neglect just
faded away and I began to heal.

Gary and I no longer live together. During this eighteen-year
marriage we have walked through the valley of shadows...but
he would always emerge on the other side of madness with a
five-gallon bottle of clean water in the back of his pick-up
truck to place in the dispenser, because he knew I couldn't lift
it anymore. In a myriad of ways, he showed me that he loved
me. He is a gifted, brilliant man...and I will always be grateful
for his many kindnesses', but Gary broke me. Years of verbal
abuse followed by days or even weeks of brooding silence.
The psychological term for this is "stone walling", and it hurts.

We explored every configuration of possibilities to save a
marriage, until finally I had to place a white flag above my
door. Gary has worked hard to overcome anger...but so much
damage has been done. I will always love him. But I can't live
with him anymore.

Owen went to school today. It is his first day of first grade.
This child has struggled with mild sensory difficulties as a
result, we think, of a cranial birth defect and corrective surgery
while still an infant. The damage is nearly imperceptible, and
he is wonderful. A beautiful, normal child with exquisite
sensitivities. He is smart, funny and interested in many things.
Daniel and Rebecca give him every opportunity to learn, grow
and explore. He and his cousin, Cora, my granddaughter, are
bright beacons of light in our lives. It is not easy to grow up in
this world...but these precious children!

She rides four-wheelers with her daddy...subtle shades of light
in her curls as they bounce over rough terrain, her beautiful
eyes flashing with amusement and wonder...

"Are you ready, Cora?" my son asks..." I ready!" she answers
jubilantly as he hoists her up in front of him. She is ready for
anything...strong and resilient and he delights in her. She will
be his salvation. (I wrote this before his tragic death, but he was
a wonderful, devoted father.)

Today, my daughter and her son drove up to the door of his Montessori school. They spare no expense as they see to Owen's needs. But several nights ago, as he lay staring at the ceiling in the darkness, he said of starting school..." What if I can't do it?" He was worried and frightened. Rebecca spoke comforting words to him...and Saturday they had a party. Children came and ate cupcakes and played like there was no tomorrow.

Then, this morning, as they sat in front of his school, Owen trying to muster the courage to enter...a dear teacher came out and took his hand and with tears flowing down his smiling face, they entered together.

He did it. The veil between courage and despair can be very thin. Today a little nuance of light shone in a dark place...and he chose courage.

Illness has taken a toll on me. Much of the feeling in my hands and feet are gone, (neuropathy, brought on by antibiotic toxicity). I am always tired, and rest doesn't restore me. I want to be well. Go to the beach again...gather shells with my grandchildren...feel salt spray on my face and sand between my toes. My mind goes to dark places as I feel myself losing ground.

But two things I can always control. I can eat healthy, healing food and live my life with integrity. It is never too late to become a good example to your children.

My friends inspire me....

Jan is a fashion plate. She is energetic, devoted, loyal, caring and beautiful. She doesn't give up on me...and gets kudos for that.

Marty has the biggest heart of anyone I have ever known...and a capacity to love that knows no bounds.

Bob has conquered agoraphobia...a demon I still wrestle with...and never stops encouraging me along my healing journey.

Peter always knows when I'm sick or sad, and never fails to call. He has shown over many years and in many ways how much he cares, and I treasure his friendship.

Jeanie is a friend indeed. She also struggles with a chronic illness but works valiantly every day to continue on as productively as her body will allow. Many days her frequent encouraging texts anchor me and keep me going. And laughter really is the best medicine!

Then there is Jay. Metastatic prostate cancer is his constant companion. He has, they say, only months to live. But his zeal for life astounds and inspires me. He still rides his motorcycle...his truest love...travels and fills his days with fascinating activities.

Next on his bucket list is a surfing expedition to Spain with his youngest son. His magnanimous heart overflows with love for his many friends...and we can feel it. He finds exquisite delight in his days, but at night I fear he sits in that easy chair overlooking the most panoramic views these mountains have to offer, and cries.

Yesterday I visited him and noticed a box of tissues sitting beside his chair. "Jay, do you sit here and cry?", I asked. He laughed, but we both knew the answer to that question. We both cry buckets of tears and most of mine are for him.

I was a cricket on the hearth with broken wings before he came. He raised me up with constant encouragement to a higher, better place. Seeing his courage gives me courage to keep striving. I am afraid I will sink back into the shadows when he is gone.

I want to reach out and help him with all that my strength allows until he is back in the hands of God...isn't that where everyone of us lies after all?

So go my days, striving to *"number them in such a way as to bring a heart of wisdom in."*
Psalm 90:12.

So go all our days...

Nothing is simply black and white. Our lives are filled with nuances of color. "Subtle differences in shades of meaning or sound...fine distinction." Fragments of light casting filigree patterns in dark places...and it is enough.

My grandchildren, Owen & Cora

Neil, Cora & Stephanie on Cora's
preschool graduation day.

Owen succeeding in school

"Let us be broken together...
That every broken heart,
Every fragment and shard,
Form one beautiful whole.
Let us be oceans of sorrow...
That we may sail beyond
All darkness...and find the beauty
Of the waiting sun on the
Far horizon...
Let us be broken together,
For broken is not dead.
It is evidence that you can feel,
And only feeling leads
To love and healing.
Today I hear you,
And any empath watching...
We have come to answer sorrow
With love...
And tell you: you are not alone...
For if a humble stranger
Can offer words of solace,
Imagine the possibilities
When the storm ends
And clouds have waned...
So, let us rise together
From the ashes
And write new stories
...Of joy and laughter.
Someone out there awaits
The gift of you, sad stranger."

Raul Gallego

"Even the small violet
Feels a future power
And waits each year
Renewing blooms to bring,
And surely man is
No inferior flower
To die unworthy
Of a second spring?"

John Clare

NANCY INGRID HURD

PASSAGES

There is a fine, misty rain this morning, and the air is cool...a welcome reprieve after days of sweltering heat. I have left my wonderful home in the mountains of North Carolina, for what could be my last visit with my mother in Pennsylvania.

She is in advanced stage dementia now and somewhere beneath the layers of amyloid plaque lies my beautiful, brilliant, funny mother. I am losing her beneath those layers and more tragic still, she is losing herself. It must be devastating.

She is pacing the floor as I descend the stairs into the kitchen.

"Who is Shana?" she asks, and I can see it upsets her that she no longer remembers. "Shana is your granddaughter", I answer quietly. "What happened to Shana?" she asks, obviously shaken. "Shana was in an accident," I say softly..." she is gone now."

"When did it happen?" she asks... "Twenty years ago," I answer.

"Twenty years" ...she repeats, sitting down at the dining room table. I sit next to her, placing my arm around her shoulders. After a pause she says, "I dreamed last night she was alive and well." "She will be again," I answer...because this is what we believe.

Before he died Jay asked me how I see myself in that promised Kingdom- where all things will be made new. This is my final text to him:

"I told you, my vision is always the same...so clear it could be a memory of real events. I see myself and my mother...young, whole, strong. Her beautiful chestnut hair, her mind clear as it was before dementia. We are walking around a quiet lake, talking and laughing as we used to do.

I see you in the distance...lean and strong...walking behind a plow...a pastural scene. We smile and wave to each other. Home is a stone house, solid as the ages...permanent as an old oak. Lace curtains are blowing in the wind. In the kitchen there is jovial talk as I cook with mother, daughter, grandmother and sister. There are "cats and babies 'round our feet and all are fat, and none are thin" like Joni Mitchell's "Ladies of the Canyon" ...wont' you come to dinner? Laughter fills the air...all stress and worry are gone. No pain or illness, like the ones ravaging my mind and your body.

Death is no more. The Keeper of Promises knows how to give back all that we have lost.

I see you there. Oh, how this dying world needs renewal. You are forever fixed in my memory like a star in the night sky. Please know you are loved. Goodbye, my friend."

This has unwittingly become a book of goodbyes...healing myself as I bury my sorrow between its pages.

Goodbye...
My beloved son
Grandma and Grandpa
Mom and Dad
Shana and Debbie
Gary and Jay
And goodbye to you too, Mark Rush, father of my
children...grandfather to our wonderful Owen and Cora. If you
could have done better, you would have done better.
I have grieved the loss of each of you here and hope that I have
touched the lives of others in the telling of it.
For those I have loved...Thank you.
For those who have loved me...Thank you.
If I hurt you, I am sorry.
If you hurt me, I forgive...I forgive...I forgive...
.... with all my heart.

Nancy Hurd   2018

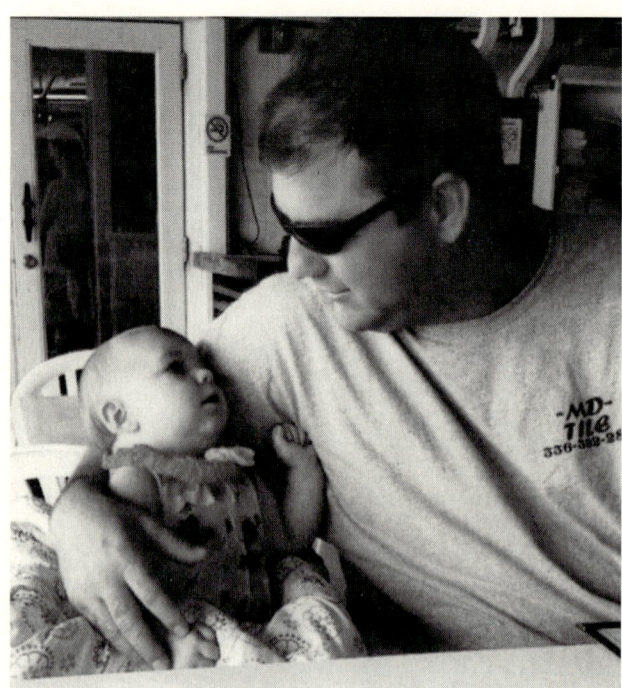

Neil & Cora

My Mother's last poem...

The Sea

By Patricia Hurd

When wild winds blow across the seas-
And billows rise and fall-
A stirring deep inside of me,
Comes the lure of an ancient call.

It surges in upon the tide,
A wind-blown voice that wails beneath
The thundering waves that beat the sand
Then end in lace that bathe my feet.

The words are distant, not distinct.
I strain my ears to catch a phrase.
A message that is meant for me
Cannot compete with roaring waves.

The sea is not a silent force;
It lives, it breathes; it reigns as king-
Over the rushing sounds that tell
The mysteries of that giant thing.

The dark depths whisper lowly-
The guarded secrets held within.
Perhaps then they relate to me-
For we must be akin.

For like the sea I heave and sigh:
I am tossed by the stormy crest.
The end of life thus waits for me-
Of silence and of rest.

And yet the sea continues on-
It washes shores around the earth,
But 'neath its roar, it murmurs low-
That each of us await rebirth.

My mother & me

"Do not wish me happiness,
For it has gone beyond that somehow.
Wish me courage, faith and a sense of humour.
For I will need all of these."

Anne Morrow Lindbergh,
From Gift from the Sea

...life is but a dream

my future...

ABOUT THE AUTHOR

Nancy was born in Fairmont, WV. to a family of coal miners, with the exception of her father, who was head of the language dept. at Waynesburg University in Southwestern PA., where she was raised. After attending university, she married and spent the next years raising her wonderful children. Although her career was in the holistic health field, she was influenced from a very early age by her mother, an avid reader and prolific and gifted writer.

Nancy resides in Asheville, NC with her husband, and is spending retirement years spoiling her grandchildren.

NANCY INGRID HURD

Made in United States
North Haven, CT
15 November 2021

11167693R00129